C0-APY-422

WE ARE

More than Conquerors

DEFEATING THE PROBLEMS OF LIFE

GLENNON CULWELL

Fair Haven Books
FairHavenBooks@gmail.com

Books By
Glennon Culwell
DEATH GOES TO SCHOOL
THE POTTER'S HANDS
PRINCES FRESSED LIKE PAUPERS
RELIGION AND POLITICS
MORE THAN CONQUERORS

Copyright © 2012 Glennon Culwell
All right reserved.
ISBN: 1470094908
ISBN: 9781470094904

IN MEMORY OF

GRANDMOTHER (Nancy) ROBERSON
AND
MYRTLE COX

Dedicated widowed saints who blessed immeasurably my ministry and the Ministry of the church known, at various times as the Valley Baptist Church, Scotts Valley Baptist Church, Granite Creek Church, currently the Gateway Bible Church. I, who came as a novice Pastor, and the church owe a debt of gratitude beyond measure to these intrepid Christian warriors of the past, of whom this church is a fulfillment of their vision.

AND FURTHER

DEDICATED TO

ALL OF THE FAITHFUL CHURCH MEMBERS

Who, over the past half century plus, have followed in the footsteps of these two dear ladies.

TABLE OF CONTENTS

WE ARE
MORE THAN CONQUERORS
DEFEATING THE PROBLEMS OF LIFE

Preface

Sitting down to write about problems and a problem-plagued world, amazingly, my mind turned to the words sung by the great *Sachmo* of jazz, Louis Armstrong, as he sang of *skies of blue and clouds of white*, concluding with the words *I think to myself, what a wonderful world!* Start to hum it and all the words will come!

You and I might make the same observation as we look upon the beauty of the world of *nature,* but then complex problems threaten that view like a raging flood, or ravaging tornado.

The world did have a wonderful beginning in every way, as God laid the foundation, *When the morning stars sang together, and all the sons of God shouted for joy.* (Job 38: 7)

But then sin established its beachhead through the disobedience of Adam, thus a veritable ocean of problems entered. Problems that seek to overwhelm us, more complex than the simple intro in the Garden called Eden, where sin entered into the world, and death passed to all men for all have sinned. (Romans 5: 12)

Now we recognize, thinking of the Sachmo again, that the skies are not always blue, for those clouds of white are often storm-clouds of problems.

The work of the Pastor/Preacher is much like that of a detective. While the detective seeks for solutions to problems from the physical world, the Pastor/Preacher, and here the Pastor/Author, searches for God's solutions to those storm-clouds of problems, from the Scriptures.

The book you hold in your hand is a record of the results of a search of some major problem(s) that attack and defeat the Christian, plaguing problems that most often rob the Christian of joy, bringing defeat to the Christian seeking to live victoriously, while being robbed of joy by the problems of daily living.

The problems may, at times, appear to be little, but like *the little foxes that spoil the vine* in Solomon's song (Song of Solomon 2: 15), they tarnish and eclipse the sun of joy in those blue skies, resulting in a defeated Christian life.

The Federal Bureau of Investigation (FBI) identifies the *10 most wanted* violators of law; and the detective may search for *public enemy number one*, desiring to arrest and take the culprit from circulation, thus removing this enemy of man from the public.

We will be dealing with the identification, arrest, and defeat of *spiritual enemy number one,* and as time and space permits, we will *sleuth* out some others, too.

However, *number one* is primary in our sights at this moment, with number two and others awaiting the author's pen!

In my book, *Princes Dressed Like Paupers*, we considered how God uses adversity, including problems, in forming our lives, *Princes dressed in rags, looking like paupers, but actually princes designed by God to help conform the believer into the image of Christ.* (Rom. 8: 28-32)

Now, the Father who uses those problems in our lives also provides solutions, for His specialty lies in the solving of the problems of life, transforming death into life, producing blessings from the blues (problems).

The fact that God came searching for Adam in the Garden, after his disobedience (Gen. 3: 9), is a clear indication of His desire to help; but Adam chose to hide and try to excuse his wrong as he passed the proverbial *buck* to his wife Eve, saying *the woman you gave me . . . .*

Now, Jesus comes on the scene seeking you, and me, saying *come to me, all you who labor and are heavy laden, and I will give you rest.* (Matthew 11: 28) Then God's word invites again, *casting all your care upon Him, for He cares for you.* (1 Pet. 5: 7), and (1 Cor. 10: 13).

But like Adam, we seek to *hide* when the Lord wants to *help* and *heal*!

Suppose we face up to our problems, begin to identify them while finding God's solutions – thus *Defeating the Problems of Life*, finding that promised ***Victory in Jesus!***

Glennon Culwell, Pastor at Large
Gateway Bible Church
Scotts Valley, California

CHAPTER ONE
SPIRITUAL ENEMY #1: THE FLESH

How to live a victorious Christian life; how to conquer daily conflicts; how to successfully deal with recurring problems that defeat
and cast one down: These are major issues faced by every Christian. Hear the apostle Paul's cry:

> *For I know that in me (that is, my flesh) nothing*
> *Good dwells; for to will is present with me, but*
> *how to perform what is good I do not find, for the*
> *good that I will to do, I do not do; but the evil I*
> *will not to do, that I practice. (Rom. 7: 18-19)*

Here is the description of the struggle of the Christian who is
endeavoring to live the victorious Christian life in the strength of
the flesh.

We find here the heart cry of every Christian trying to live the
Christian life in the flesh; crying out to be free of this constant inner
conflict that defeats and robs him of the joy for which he searches.

The individual becomes a Christian, feeling that everything will
be *rosy*, perhaps thinking that he will be *carried to the skies on flow-
ery beds of ease,* only to fall into the depths of despair in the raging
conflict between flesh and spirit, visited by a mass of problems like
a swarm of yellow jackets attacking a picnic lunch!

The Holy Spirit bears witness to the spirit of the individual that
He lives within, that the individual is a child of God's (Romans 8:
16); but *why,* then, the rending conflict that persistently casts him
down, robbing him of joy like John Dillinger after the First National
Bank?

1

What is the solution? That there is one, you may be sure, and here is the purpose of, not only this chapter, but the entire book: *How to Defeat the Problems of Life.*

The first problem faced by the Christian is that of the *flesh*, like a continual tug of war, man strives for dominance over the old, natural man.

Here are some vital truths, if we are to be free of the flesh:

THE SAMENESS IN FEELINGS

The Christian hurts just the same as the unbeliever when he is injured. He bleeds just like anyone else when he is wounded. His blood is the same color.

He, or she, does not suddenly become *Super-man* or *Wonder-woman*, a super-saint, soaring supersonically skyward above the pains of the world.

The Christian will avoid much heartache if he or she will only realize with the Psalmist, *Lord, that I may know how frail I am!* (Ps. 39: 4), or as we hear from the lips of the prophet Isaiah, *All flesh is grass*, as he continues by saying it *withers and fails.*

Christians struggle and fail, crying out, why is this happening to me? They have forgotten that they still have the *same* body of flesh, mortal, death-doomed. The Bible speaks of man being *mortal,* that word coming from the Greek *thanitos,* meaning *liable to death.*

IN TEMPTATIONS

The believer faces the same temptations as everyone else. The nature of the flesh is to *lust.*

For the flesh lusts against the spirit . . . . (Gal. 5: 17)

Much heartbreak would be avoided if Christians would realize this truth. Yet, they cry out, as they seem to be going down for the third time in the seas of sin and temptations. *I don't understand why I do these things, that is, have these desires. . . .*

2

I'm reminded of the old joke about the three preachers visiting together in a hotel room while attending a convention. They decided to share their problems, as the first one said, *My weakness is money. I just can't keep from dipping my hand into the offering plate.* The second preacher said, *My weakness is women. I can't resist an attractive woman.* The third quickly responded, *My weakness is gossip and I can hardly wait to get out of this room to a phone!*

Now, after a little laugh, we should become somber, realizing that the tendency of the flesh remains the same, and that there is a continual warfare of the spirit with the flesh.

We quoted just the first part of Galatians 5:17 that said *the flesh lusts against the [Holy] Spirit*, but failed to continue by reading, *and the spirit against the flesh. . . .*, as the inspired writer continues, *and these are contrary to one another, that you do not do the things you wish.* (Gal. 5: 17)

We must recognize that the tendency of the flesh remains the same after conversion, being called *the old man* in the Scriptures, thus conflict is a natural result.

Before I really yielded my life to Christ, I guzzled beer and loved it. So, what do you think would come to my mind on a hot, dry summer's day? You are right! A cold, frosty bottle of Budweiser would flash on the screen of my mind. Shirley Cheek, wife of my mentor and devoted Christian friend, had the same taste as I did in the *old days* – of *the old man . . . .* On a hot Texas day, she and I would laugh, saying, *wouldn't a cold bottle of beer taste good?*

The flesh has the same potential it had before conversion. Sin is still appealing and enjoyable to the flesh. We need to realize this truth in order to build out spiritual defenses, in order that, when the cold bottle of Bud *flashes across the screen of my flesh, I find myself a good, cold glass . . . of iced tea!*

SOME PROBLEMS

The problems faced by the Christian also remain the same. The world about us remains essentially unchanged, only our view toward it changes – or should.

The pressures of living, the stresses of the job or business, the problems of a problem-ridden, corrupt society continue.

Here is the issue: You have found that Jesus Christ has saved you from the *penalty* of sin, but you have not found Him as Savior from the *power* of sin. Is deliverance from sin's *penalty* the only deliverance that the Lord Jesus offers? Are we expected to just settle down to a life of alternate triumphs and defeats, one hour sinning, the next serving; one moment cast down, the next lifted up? Is this all that the *new life* offers?

No, no, no! *We are more than conquerors, through Him who loved us.* (Rom. 8: 37) Ours is not a bankrupt inheritance that alternates between wounded transgressions, bruised iniquities, and abundant life – spiritual schizophrenia!

We started out considering Paul's cry of conflict in Romans, chapter seven, doing what he didn't want to do, and not doing what he wanted. Considering this conflict between law and grace, he cries out, *O wretched man that I am! Who will deliver me from this body of death (mortal, death doomed flesh)?* (Romans 7: 24)

He answers his own question with a shout of glory. *I thank God – through Jesus Christ our Lord! So then, with the mind I myself serve the law of God, but with the flesh the law of sin.* (Rom. 7: 25). *Who will deliver me?* Paul asked. His answer, *I thank God – through Jesus Christ our Lord* – He delivers!

HOW THE CHRISTIAN DIFFERS

Therefore, if anyone is in Christ he is a new creation . . . (II Cor. 5: 17).

HE HAS A SAVIOR

The Christian is different, unique, because he has a Savior. The angel, announcing the birth of the Savior to Joseph, said of our Savior's work, *He will save His people from their sins.* (Mt 1: 21). Zacharias, filled with the Holy Spirit, said that, *we, being delivered from the hand of our enemies, might serve Him . . .* (Luke: 1: 74).

Paul, writing to Titus, said that the Savior gave himself that *He might redeem us from every lawless deed.* (Titus 2: 14).

He saved us, redeeming us from the *power* of sin. Thus, we see the inconsistency of continuing to be in subjection to sin!

Suppose your small child were kidnapped, and you redeemed him, (paying a ransom for his freedom), but the kidnapper continues holding him in bondage. You would not consider that a very successful transaction, would you?

Well, Christ ransomed us, not only from the *penalty* of sin, but also from the *power* of sin. Will we, then, degrade that transaction by remaining in bondage to sin's power?

HE HAS HOPE

The believer is different because he has hope. David said, *The Lord is my rock and my fortress and my deliverer; the God of my strength in whom I will trust; my shield and the horn of my salvation; my stronghold and my refuge; my Savior, You save me from violence.* (II Sam. 22: 2-3).

Setting apart just a couple of the figures of speech that David credits to the character of God, I think of what it means to say that God is his *shield.* I see David facing his enemy, holding a shield before himself for protection against the enemy's arrows. Thus, He is our shield of faith with which we will be able to *quench all the fiery darts of the wicked one.* (Eph. 6: 16).

Or take his figure when He says that God is *my refuge*, which reminds us of his statement in the 46th Psalm, *God is our refuge and strength, a very present help in trouble.*(v. 1). Thus, we can, *Call to [Him]* as God says, *and I will show you great and mighty things, which you do not know* (Jer. 33: 3); and when you walk through the valley of shadows, He is with you (Ps. 23: 1). You are not left alone to face those dark hours. As the poet has written in a great, old hymn,

I've found a friend, oh, such a friend!
He loved me ere I knew Him,
He drew me with the chords of love,
and thus He bound me to Him;
and round my heart still closely twine
those cords which naught can sever,
for I am His and He is mine,
forever, and forever.

Yes, we've found a friend like no other, thus we are now different because we have a Savior! We have this promise, *When you pass through the waters, I will be with you; and through the rivers; they shall not overthrow you. When you walk through the fire, you shall not be burned, nor shall the flame scorch you. For I am your God, the Holy One of Israel, your Savior.* (Isaiah 43: 2-3)

When we pass through the waters of temptations, they will not overflow and overwhelm; when we go through fiery trials and problems, we will not be consumed. He is with us!

Yes, we believers are different because we have a *presence* and *power*, as He said,

I will never leave you nor forsake you.
So we boldly say, The Lord is my helper;
I will not fear. What can man do to me?
(Heb. 13: 5-6)

CONCLUSION

I love the figure of God as the potter. Perhaps you have read my book *The Potter's Hands*, in which I traced how God, the Potter, molded my life. We will be seeing the Potter appear throughout this book!

The Potter provides the principle with which we close this chapter.

We recognize that, if the flesh is to be neutralized and defeated, it will be the Potter who makes it possible, for it is the Potter and not the clay (flesh) who is responsible for forming the finished product.

The Potter's part is to do the molding. The clay's part is simply to trust and yield to the touch of the Potter.

> *He touched me, O He touched me,*
> *And O the joy that floods my soul.*
> *Something happened, and now I know*
> *He touched me, and made me whole.*

CHAPTER ONE

STUDY/DISCUSSION GUIDE

1. Put the Apostle Paul's words found in Romans 7: 13-24 in your own words, personalize them, and then discuss their meaning.

2. What do we mean when we say the Christian is *"the same"*?

3. Name the ways the believer is the same as anyone else (Psalm 39: 4, I Peter 1: 24).

4. What does it mean to say that *"man is mortal"*?

5. Does our flesh *lust*, and if so, in what way? Can you share an area of your life that has troubled you?

CHAPTER TWO

SPIRITUAL ENEMY #1, THE FLESH

STEPS IN DEFEATING THE FLESH

Do you live a completely victorious Christian life? Few believers can answer that question with an unqualified *yes*. *Yes,* we might answer, at times my life is victorious; but isn't it true that the majority of believer's lives are characterized more by *defeat*, trapped like a raccoon caught stealing the bait from a bear's trap?

We considered, just briefly, the solution to our problem in the past chapter, illustrated in the words of this beautiful old hymn by N. V. Clayton,

> *Only to be what He wants me to be,*
> *every moment of every day;*
> *yielded completely to Jesus alone,*
> *every step of the pilgrim way;*
> *just to be* **clay in the Potter's hands**,
> *ready to do what the Lord commands,*
> *only to be what He wants me to be,*
> *every moment of every day.*

It was here that we found a vital principle that *must be known and followed*, that is, if we are to live the abundant life. God is to do the work; man's part is to *yield* himself to God, *yielded completely to Jesus alone,* as the poet wrote. God is the Potter; man is the clay. The clay does not do the molding. That is the Potter's job. The clay can only yield itself completely to the Potter, being pliable in every part.

Then the Potter molds, applying pressure: pains, blessings, divine influences, all used in making the vessel into a finished product, fit for the Potter's use, *just to be clay in the Potter's hands, ready to do what the Lord commands.*

Taking Romans, chapter six as our source in this chapter, we will recognize *the steps to* be taken in obtaining victory over the flesh, the formula for a victorious life.

THE FIRST STEP
We begin by reading and applying Romans 6: 6 to our lives.

> *. . . knowing this, that our old man was crucified with Him, that the body of sin might be done away with, that we should no longer be slaves of sin.*

Knowing this, marks the first step. Because I know, I desire; because I know, I do; because I know, I will. It is the *unknown* that defeats us. Man is inherently afraid of the unknown.

On the other hand, you talk to God because you *know* Him. You go to Him because He *knows* the way you should take, since He *is the way.* (John 14: 6). But we fail to go because we don't trust, because we fail to know that He is a God of love, a God of mercy.

Jesus said,

> *What man is there among you who, if his son asks for bread, will give him a stone? Or if he asks for a fish, will he give him a serpent? If you then, being evil, **know** how to give good gifts to your children, how much more will your Father who is in heaven, give good things to those who ask Him? (Mt. 7: 10, 11)*

The issue is *knowing.* If you know what an earthly father will give, you can *know* how much more your heavenly Father will give!

Here is a reason Christians are defeated in the self life, in the flesh. They know the lusts of the flesh, but don't know by experience, the love of the Father.

WHAT ARE WE TO KNOW?

What are we to know? In general we are to know that the Lord Jesus Christ has taken care of the problem of *self*, of the flesh, the greatest obstacle to the faith life.

Our inspired writer has asked that we know, in this order: *Our old man [of the flesh] was* **crucified with Him** . . . as Paul phrases this truth in Galatians 2: 24, *I have been crucified with Christ . . .* He has taken self out of the way, nailing it to the cross, putting it to death. Consequently, if self is dead it cannot lust!

Next, he wants us to *know what the purpose* of this death is, *that the body of sin might be done away* (be rendered inoperative) – absolutely imperative if the self-life is dead and powerless.

The final thing He wants us to *know* about our identification with Christ's death is: Knowing that He has put self to death, he then knows that, he who has died *has [also] been freed from sin.* (Romans 6: 7)

We need to know, by experience (*ginowsko*), that we have been *crucified with Christ*, the Lord having dealt with and provided a solution for the flesh, or *self,* consequently the sin problem. When we are convinced of this truth, know it by experience, we will have taken the first step on our journey to victory.

John Wesley set out to gain a right relationship with God by obeying a strict set of rules. Then he met the God of grace through His Son Jesus at Aldersgate Street on May 24, 1738. He said regarding *self, An assurance was given me that He (Christ) had taken away **my** sins, even mine, and saved me from the law of sin and death.*

His brother Charles, having become a great hymn writer, expressed the same truth in a hymn.

> *I felt the Lord's atoning blood*
> *Close to my soul applied;*

Me, Me He loved – the Son of God,
For me, for me He died.

THE SECOND STEP

The second step can be summarized by the word **trust**. The key is found in the eleventh verse of Romans, chapter six,

*Likewise you also **reckon** yourselves to be dead indeed to sin, but alive to God in Christ our Lord.*

RECKON

When you **reckon** self to be dead, you are affirming the truth to yourself that your old sin-life died on the cross. Remember in Galatians 2: 20, Paul wrote, *I am crucified with Christ.* Note, then, that he goes ahead to say, *and the life I now live in the flesh* (a new kind of flesh-life) *I live by faith in the Son of God, who loved me and gave Himself for me.*

To reckon is to affirm **by faith**, with action accompanying, that you consider self to be dead to sin. Just as James would write, *Faith without works [accompanying action] is dead.* (James 21: 24)

Note that, upon this step being taken by you, it is the Spirit Who puts the flesh life to death. This truth is clearly expressed in Romans 8:13, *if by the Spirit you put to death the deeds of the body, you will live.*

We are to permit the Lord to take care of our problems, manage our affairs for us instead of trying to do it ourselves. After all, that's what it means when we call Him Lord.

I am reminded of a young man, sort of a *hippie type,* that I picked up hitchhiking. He was carrying a big sack of odds and ends he had been gathering to sell. Carrying the bag in his lap, I suggested that he rest it on the floor. Just suppose after I suggested that he put his load down and rest, that he had answered, *Oh no, I can't do that. It's enough just asking you to carry me, much less my burden, too.*

So it is that Christians continue to bear their own problems, burdened and heavy-laden, all the while Christ wants them to trust

Him, to *reckon* the death of their problems, permitting Him to bear them.

He made you, understands you, and knows how to make the best of every area of your life. You need to trust Him like a small child trusts his parents. Think about the characteristics of a child. He lives by faith in his parents, and is free of care. He trusts his parents to meet every need and solve every problem. The small child provides nothing for himself, yet everything is provided. Wars may rage; riots may foment in the streets; the value of the dollar may decline and plunge; the stock market may falter; but under his parents' care and concern, the child remains in perfect peace!

God is called Father; we are called His children. The Lord is called Shepherd; we are called sheep. His desire is to gather us together and care for us like a shepherd cares for his sheep.
Why do God's children not trust Him in such a fashion? It seems as though they do not really *know* Him, and that they are afraid of His will, as though He is going to punish them for trusting Him.

What if your child were to come to you saying, I love you and I want to obey you, and do everything to please you – everything you want me to do, whatever you think best. Would you say, Aha, now I have an opportunity to make him miserable. I'm going to take away all of his toys and put him on a diet of bread and water. From now on I'm making him sleep on the hard floor, making him as uncomfortable as possible. I'm going to find every distasteful task I can find and make him do it.

Would you do that? Oh, no. You would take him in your arms, love him, and give him your sweetest and best.

Well then, do you love more than God? We reject God's will for our lives as though, if we submit, He will immediately visit us with the plague and think up the most distasteful and miserable things to do to us.

If the child asks for a fish, will a father give him a scorpion? How much more will your heavenly Father give good gifts to those who ask Him!

The first step on our journey to victory over the flesh: **know** Christ and what He has already done for you; the second step: **trust** the Lord to give you victory – **reckon** self dead.

YIELD YOURSELVES

The third step, say *no* to self and **yield** yourselves to God, and yield your members as instruments of righteousness to God (Romans 6: 13, KJV). I like this translation in the King James Version, although the New King James translates it *present yourselves to God.*

Perhaps we could put the two together and say, *yield* the right of way of your life to God, and *present* yourself to Him. Oh, I'm just playing with words: Yield or present. The word *yield* seems to be reminding us that God has a plan for our life. We say *no* to self and *yield* to Him, and accept His plan. Otherwise, the word *present* seems to emphasize that you take the initiative . . . Do either, and you get the total picture!

Here is the Potter–clay principle again. Our part is to yield, submit, present, and He takes and molds what we *freely* give. We yield, submit, present and resolve to make every area of life pliable in His hands, and He molds!

What if we stumble in the process and a flaw appears? Do we have to remove the flaw ourselves? No, we just keep on yielding, and the Potter removes the flaw. (I John 1: 9)

The key is to just keep on yielding, keep on submitting, keep on presenting – so as to always be pliable to the touch of the Father's hands. *He touched me, and made me whole,* wrote the poet.

YIELD EVERYTHING!

We would be remiss if we failed to deal with the balance of this verse and its admonition. We are told . . . *do not present your members as instruments of unrighteousness to sin, but present . . . your members as instruments of righteousness to God.* (Romans 6: 13)

First, we present or yield self, the greatest problem we face. Next, we yield or present our *members,* everything and every part that goes together in making *self.*

Here is the point at which we fail. We say we submit, but then specify exceptions. *Lord, **I'm yours** to command. Then we say, here is **my plan** for making me into what* I want to be. Or we say, *Lord, I'll give you everything **but**. . .* and you can fill in the blank. Right now, what is that secret thing that you reserve from your commitment to His Lordship?

Suppose you go to the doctor and say, *Doctor, I want you to take my case and cure me. However, I want to prescribe my own medications; and here is the plan I want you to follow; and, by the way, there are some infected, poisonous, cancerous members I want you to leave alone.*

What do you think the doctor would do? You know the answer. If you will not submit, yield yourself into his hands and trust his treatment, he'll tell you to go elsewhere.

I remember receiving a telephone call during the wee hours of the morning years ago. A young man had been seriously injured in an automobile wreck in the Palo Alto area, and the lady calling desperately needed transportation to get there to sign consent before the surgeon would operate. He would not operate without consent.

So it is that God requires our *consent* before operating on our lives. We must *yield*, place ourselves into His hands, *trusting* His plans and prescriptions, willing that He makes of every area of life what He wants it to be.

HOW ABOUT YOU?

Some of you may say, *I have done this and I'm **not** pleased with the results, that is, with what God has made of me. I had other plans; but He seemed to have alternate plans along the way. My venture with God has been a failure.*

One must be reminded that God's plans are perfect at every step along the way. Thinking of a peach tree, its fruit in June is the best fruit June can produce; but that fruit is very different from the fruit in August, which, at that point is mature and ripe.

If you are truly trusting and yielded, do not be displeased with the type and size of vessel God has made, and its function, but be content that it is made for His use and glory!

He bestows the gifts, and equips us to use them. Do not disparage your gift. If He gives you, say, the gift of *helps* as a helper, instead of a more glamorous gift of leadership you may have coveted, permit Him to make of you a perfect helper!

OBEDIENCE

There is yet another step along the path of victory, the step of **obedience**. *Do you not know that to whom you present yourselves slaves to **obey**, you are that one's slaves you obey, whether of sin leading to death, or of **obedience leading to righteousness**.* (Rom. 6: 16)

Remember, a vessel is molded for a purpose: the cup for drinking, the pitcher for pouring. The Potter's purpose for us is that we serve, bringing much fruit and glory to the Potter. He does not mold us so we can sit on the shelf and say *Look at me. For we are His workmanship, created in Christ Jesus unto good works, which God has ordained that we should walk in them.* (Eph. 2: 10)

Even here our work depends on Him. We function as an instrument in His hands, trusting and yielding to be used by Him. Like a scalpel is an instrument in the surgeon's hand, so we are an instrument in the Master Surgeon's hand. Did you ever see a scalpel making its own incision, free of the surgeon's hand? How would you like to have a scalpel operate on you? The apostle wrote,

> *I labored; yet not I, but the grace of God*
> *which was with me.*

How can we have this victorious quality of life? We cannot earn it; we cannot climb to get it; though we have a ladder reaching to heaven; it is ours in response to faith, for the taking.

The steps to the life of victory over the flesh: **know** what the Lord Jesus has done for you; **reckon** yourself dead to sin; **yield** yourself into God's hands; **obey** by being willing to be used as an instrument in the Master's hands.

The story is told of a visitor walking along a high point along the shores of the Dead Sea, when he lost his footing and fell into the water. He could not swim and, in desperation, lest he sink and drown, he began to fling his arms and legs about. At last, exhausted, he could struggle no more. Then something strange happened as he relaxed. The water in the Dead Sea is so heavy with salt and minerals that, when he relaxed he floated! He could not drown as long as he committed himself to the water.

And so it is: we cannot be defeated by the flesh as long as we commit ourselves to the Savior and depend fully on Him.

George Muller serves as an excellent example of one who perfectly followed the steps recognized in Romans, Chapter six which we have just considered. Muller is renowned for caring for thousands of orphan children, and raising over a million pounds in paying for their care, all by faith! He wrote in his autobiography, *George Muller of Bristol*:

There was a day when I died, utterly died. . . .died to George Muller, his opinions, preferences, tastes and will; died to the world, its approval or blame even of my brethren and friends and, since then, I have studied only to show myself approved to God.

George Muller could truly say with the Apostle Paul that *I am crucified with Christ* and that *it is no longer I who live, but Christ Who lives in me.* (Galatians 2: 20)

Follow the steps outlined above and you are in a position to make the same claim!

STUDY/ DISCUSSION GUIDE, CHAPTER TWO

STEPS IN DEFEATING THE FLESH

1. What is the first step in defeating the flesh, leading to the victorious Christian life? (Rom. 6: 6; Gal. 2: 20a)

2. What are you to know? Answer and discuss.

3. What validates knowledge? (Gal. 2: 20b)

4. What is the second step to the victorious life? (Rom. 6: 11)

5. What does the word *reckon* mean, and what is suggested that the believer is to do? (Rom. 8: 13)

6. Why do God's children not trust Him? Answer and discuss.

7. What is the third step to victory? (Rom. 6: 13)

8. Name similar words for the word *yield,* and suggested meanings, and how they impact this admonition.

9. Following the analogy of the Potter and clay, what is the role of the clay? What is the role of the Potter? Are the roles inter-changeable? Discuss.

10. What is meant by *yield . . . your members . . .?* (Rom. 6: 13)

11. What is the fourth step in accomplishing victory? (Rom. 6: 16; Eph 2: 10)

CHAPTER THREE

SPIRITUAL ENEMY #1, THE FLESH

VICTORY BY ENLARGING YOUR VIEW OF GOD

As we think about living victoriously in defeating the problems of life, we have realized that, to do so one must *yield* his life, his body (every member) into the hands of God, like clay in the Potter's hand; and then must *trust* Him implicitly to make of his life what the Potter desires, in full assurance that the very best will result.

That's a tall order! So, we can rightly ask, how is such yieldedness and trust possible?

First, you must get your eyes fastened on something bigger than our giant, egocentric self, something or *someone* who doesn't represent failure.

We look to man, as unstable as a bowl of Jell-O, or like a feather in the wind, as he shifts like an NFL running-back endeavoring to escape the hands of muscle-bound linemen, only to be tackled by a line-backer - *failure*. Who is it who has never wept over the failure of lover or friend? Oh, the giant-failures of man!

So, first, you must get your eyes off of men.

We have looked at the material things of life, thinking, *If I can only have a nest-egg in the bank, a house of my own, or a good retirement plan . . . ;* yet, who is it who has had it all and then been crushed by failures in the material realm? The nest-egg has its shell cracked by a stock-market decline; the dream house has been undermined by termite debts or blown away on the storms of poverty.

I think of my own dad who worked so hard to achieve such dreams, achieving many of them. He retired at the age of 65; ready to enjoy the fruit of his dreams, but literally days later had those dreams disappear like the sun behind a storm-cloud, as he died from a terminal malignancy. If we want to trust, we must get our eyes off of the flesh and material things of life.

How about just turning to the illusive dream of *pleasure*, eat, drink, and be merry, one might ask? Yet, we eat and it turns to cholesterol in the bloodstream; we drink and a hangover of cirrhosis drowns our pleasures in a sea of sickness.

No, if we want to have a trust that satisfies and survives the ravages of time, we must get our eyes off of pleasure.

Finally, if we really want to trust, as we found earlier, we must get our eyes set on something big, something that does not crumble like a house filled with fleshly desires, on Jesus!

Thus, if we are to truly trust God, as the Potter to mold our lives, we must *yield* our lives as a pliable vessel into His hands, for we know that *He will not fail,* filling the vessel with flaws; nor will He drop it, to be broken and cast upon the trash-heap of life!

With this in mind, let us focus on His *trustworthiness*.

THE WORK OF THE POTTER'S HANDS

First, we get a glorious glance at His capabilities, as the Psalmist records in that majestic eighth Psalm,

O Lord, our God
how excellent is your name
in all the earth,
who have set your glory
above the heavens

. . . . .

when I consider your heavens
the work of your fingers,
the moon and the stars,
which you have ordained . . .
(Psalm 8: 1, 3)

God created the universe, in all of its fullness and perfections, with its myriads of galaxies.

> *He stretched out the north over empty space;*
> *He hangs the earth on nothing.*
> *He binds up the water in His thick clouds,*
> *yet the clouds are not broken under it.*
> *He covers the face of His throne,*
> *and spreads His cloud over it.*
> *He drew a circular horizon on the face*
> *of the waters at the boundary of light and darkness.*
> *The pillars of heaven tremble, and are*
> *astonished at His rebuke.*
> *He stirs up the sea with His power.*
> *And by His understanding, He breaks up the storm.*
> *By His spirit He adorned the heavens.*
> *His hand pierced the fleeing serpent.*
> *Indeed, these are the mere edges of His ways,*
> *and how small a whisper we hear of Him!*
> *But the thunder of His power who can understand?*
> *(Job 26: 7-13)*

Just meditate on the greatness of His creation, and we see His greatness and omnipotence. He framed our days with the glorious sunrise and the breathless sunset. Our eyes delight as we stand in awe of the towering mountain peaks and the crashing of the ocean waves. We are overwhelmed by the majesty of the heaven above, which stretches from horizon to horizon, studded with myriads of stars.

The Psalmist said, *When I consider your heavens . . .* But the tragedy: so few trust *because* they have never really paused to meditate on the glory of God's creation.

The story is told by a traveler who came upon a tribe of *moon-worshippers* in his travels. He expressed surprise at their preference, expecting that they would have chosen the sun. Why such a choice, the traveler inquired. *The sun shines foolishly in the day-time when there is plenty of light,* they replied. *The moon conveniently shines at night when it is dark!*

The tribe, not realizing that the moon's light was a mere reflection of the sun, lost sight of the greater light! All too often we are like these *moon-worshippers,* missing seeing God's greater glory as we squabble with the sparrows scrambling for the crumbs of the world.

A thoughtless person once said to Helen Keller, the blind and deaf darling of her world, *Isn't it awful to be blind?* Helen replied *Not half so bad as to have two good eyes and never see anything.* We have heard of the little boy who was rebuked for his grammatical error saying *I seen.* He replied, *Better to say 'I seen' and see something, than 'I seen' and never see anything.*

I recall the time when my boys, Christian and Andrew, had a couple of small turtles in a little plastic tank. Those turtles never knew the beauty of the heavens, the exhilaration of the great out-of-doors. They never saw beyond their little tank. It was their world.

So it is with man, seldom really seeing beyond the four walls of his house, the confines of his job, the circumference of the people around him, content with that small view. So sad that many fail to consider the heavens and work of God's hands, for *The heavens declare the glory of God; and the firmament (the work of His hands) shows His handiwork.* (Psalm 19: 1)

WHEN YOU CONSIDER GOD'S CREATION

Two things happen when one really stops to consider and becomes conscious of the greatness of God's creation.

First, he realizes that our God is truly indescribably great. While in Waikiki, I marveled at the greatness of some high-rises constructed by Donald Trump, which replaced, in part, the location of mine and my wife's favorite restaurant. My wife Jean and I rode to the top of the Empire State Building on our honeymoon, a trip that required a change in elevators it was so high. We marveled at its height, and then stared at Manhattan's skyline in awe. We climbed to the crown of the Statue of Liberty, and were amazed.

Yet, all of that pales into insignificance when compared to *the heavens [that] declare the glory of God.* Years ago I copied a newspaper article about a polar eclipse on June 30, 1973. The article reported that the eclipse, lasting only 7.2 minutes, would be repeated 213 years later in 2186, and again at that time would last exactly 7.2 minutes. So precise was the movement of heavenly bodies, as created by the hand of God, that an event will take place 213 years later at exactly the same second in time!

If we can only depend on the sun to rise at a precise moment tomorrow, and dispel the darkness, we can depend on the God of the sun to dispel the darkness in our lives, and can trust Him to make of us what we ought to be.

We need to see a great God, the God of creation, one who not only has time but eternity in His hands. Then, in the light of His great love for us, we will realize that He is able to take care of any and all problems that beset us!

> *When I consider your heavens, the work*
> *of your fingers . . . what is man that you are*
> *mindful of him, and the Son of Man that you*
> *visit him? (Psalm 8: 3, 4)*

Second, when we consider the greatness of God's creation, we are compelled to think big thoughts! *When I* **consider** *. . . ,* and at that moment in time we are caused to *think*, and as we think we see the greatness of God in comparison to our puny persona!

What are your thoughts as you view creation? Two men were looking out a window after a rainstorm. One said, *Just look at the mud in the street.* The other said, *The stars are shining beautifully.* Perhaps we should re-think Sachmo Louis Armstrong's words*, what a wonderful world* – which tells us of its wonderful Creator!

Failure results when we lose sight of the greatness of God.

Now, what we have written and read causes us to look beyond the Creator, and look at

GOD HIMSELF

Here we are confronted by a problem seemingly as big as the sky above, yet the solution is well in our grasp. How can we see and understand God? How can our finite minds ever comprehend an infinite God?

The problem is solved by God's revelation of Himself, through the person and personality of His Son, our Lord Jesus Christ, Who in turn gives us the *victory!* The Apostle Paul wrote, *O wretched man that I am! Who will deliver me from the body of this death? I thank God – **through Jesus Christ our Lord!***

Jesus said, *He who has seen me has seen the Father . . .* (John 14: 9) Again, the inspired writer of the letter to the Hebrews wrote concerning Jesus:

You, Lord, in the beginning
laid the foundation of the earth,
And the heavens are the work
of Your hands. (Hebrews 1: 10)

Our Lord Jesus is the express image of God's person, as we read again; *He [Jesus] is the image of the invincible God, the first born over all creation.* (Colossians 1: 15)

One can only see and understand God, when you see, know, and understand the Christ. How one sees God depends on his or her relationship and view of the Savior, because He is God revealed in the form of flesh. *He who has seen Me has seen the Father,* the Master said to Philip, in answer to Philip's request, *Lord, show us the Father, and it is sufficient for us.* (John 13: 8, 9).

What do you see when you see Jesus? Permit me to tell you what I see:

One, I see God taking the form of human flesh, *Emmanuel, God with us* (Isaiah 14: 7), conceived by the Holy Spirit, born of a virgin. Consequently, He was born free of the poison of sin which had been handed down through the first man, Adam. God took this form in order that we might see and know Him.

Two, when I see Jesus [by faith as revealed in God's word], I see a perfect life which *was in all points tempted as we are yet without sin.* (Heb. 4: 15) He lived a flawless life so as to make the same kind of life available to the *whosoevers* who trust Him as Savior.

Man, within himself, is death-doomed, for *There is none who does good, no, not one* (Rom. 3:12), *for the wages of sin is death* (Rom. 6: 23). Christ alone was free of sin's dominion, having lived that quality of life in order that He now *imputes righteousness apart from works.* (Rom. 4: 6) – without man's help!

Three, when I see Jesus, I see a God of perfect justice, who paid the penalty of sin *for us*, a *substitute* for us as He suffered and died. *For He [God] made Him who knew no sin to be sin for us, that we might become the righteousness of God in Him.* (2 Cor. 5: 21)

Here I see an innocent, matchless, incomparable Savior, Who was beaten, thorn-pierced, suffering on the cross, the cruelest form of execution. I see that tortured body, hanging between two thieves, hanging by nail-pierced hands and feet on that cursed tree; and I hear Him crying in agony, *My God, My God, why, why have you forsaken me?* (Mt. 27: 46) I see His head fall forward in death as He cries, *It is finished.* I see the Roman centurion plunge his spear into His side, blood and water flowing down from His broken heart. It is here that I see Him, after He has tasted death, being laid away in a tomb.

The words of the Prophet Isaiah are now fulfilled: *wounded for our transgressions; bruised for our iniquities, cut off out of the land of the living; oppressed and afflicted; led as a lamb to the slaughter; and the Lord has laid on Him the iniquity of us all.* (Isaiah 53)

Four, I see one whose power is greater than death, for the grave could not hold Him, as the Bible says, *why seek the living among the dead? He is not here, but is risen.* (Luke 24: 5, 6) The embodiment of eternal life and its source – *In Him was life . . .* (John 1: 7)

I see God who *was not willing that any should perish, but that all should come to repentance.* (II Peter 3: 9)

APPLICATION

Do you want to be able to *trust* and *yield*, in order that flesh is defeated, becoming as obedient as a slave to his master?

> *If so, Turn your eyes upon Jesus, look full*
> *in His wonderful face; and the things of earth*
> *Will grow strangely dim, in the light of His glory*
> *and grace.*

CHAPTER THREE

STUDY AND DISCUSSION GUIDE

1. What are the two things one must do to have victory over the problems of life? One must_____his life, and _____ God.

2. Changing your view of life, you must first get your eyes off of _____. Discuss what this entails.

3. Next, you must get your eyes on something _____ than you. Discuss.

4. Discuss the work of God. (Psalm 8: 1, 3), (Job 26: 7- 13)

5. What two things happen when you consider God's creation? (a) We realize that God is _____. Discuss.

   (b) We are compelled to _____ big. (Psalm 8: 3, 4)

6. How can we see and understand God? (John 14: 9; Hebrews 1:1- 3; Colossians 1: 15). Discuss.

7. Do you remember what I see when I see Jesus? (Isaiah 7: 14; Hebrews 4: 15; 2 Corinthians 5: 21; 2 Peter 3: 9) Discuss.

8. Put into your own words what you see when you see Jesus.

9. How will you apply this lesson to yourself?

CHAPTER FOUR

SPIRITUAL ENEMY #1: THE FLESH

VICTORY BY ENLARGING THE VIEW OF YOURSELF

I'm no good. I'm not worth anything. I'm like a speck of dust on a sandy beach. How could God ever use such a miserable creature like me? I'm just no good, not worth the powder it would take to blow me up. How many times have you heard words such as these, even from the mouth of Christians? They feel as worthless as a lead nickel in a twenty-five cent jukebox, as undependable as a Russian airliner*! I'm just a poor, weak worm of the dust.*

What is the true value of self? There are those who see no value inherently in man. Benjamin Disraeli, twice Prime Minister of England, reviewing his life concluded *Youth is a mistake; manhood is a struggle; old age a regret.* Jay Gould, An early American multimillionaire capitalist, evaluated his life in these words: *I suppose I am the most miserable devil on earth.*

To suggest that man is worthless, as suggested in these examples, contradicts the word of God and besmirches God's creation. Upon concluding His six days of creation, concluding with the creation of man, God saw that what He had created was *very good!* (Genesis 1: 31)

Still others see man as having absolute, supreme value apart from God, denying the truth of creation and that there is even a Creator. For example, Protagoras cried, *Man is a measure of all things.* Henley blatantly proclaimed:

I am the master of my fate;
I am the captain of my soul.

What is the truth? What is the true value of man? That he has great value cannot be questioned, being so highly valued by God that He gave *His only begotten Son* in redeeming him from sin. Yet, man is obviously flawed, as we read from the Scriptures:

There is none righteous, no not one;
there is none who understands; there is
none who seeks after God. They have all
turned aside; they have together become
unprofitable; there is none who does good,
no not one.

Yet, what if I continue to say that man is not worthless, but rather is of great value? In light of what has just been said, such a statement seems as contradictory as an Indian chief smoking a peace-pipe while scalping a pale-face!

Yet, such is precisely what I am saying. Individual man is of incalculable, immeasurable, incomprehensible value! — as seen through the eyes of God. *What is man that You are mindful of him, and the son of man that You visit him? For You have made him a little lower than the angels, and You have crowned him with glory and honor. You have made him to have dominion over the works of Your hands.* (Psalm 8: 4-6)

We have considered defeating the problems of life by enlarging our view of God; **now let us consider defeating the problems of life by enlarging our view of self.**

Our purpose, in this chapter, is to get you to see yourself in a better light, to have a higher esteem of yourself; your worth and capabilities. Man will never succeed if he has a debased value of himself, often expressed in a sense of false humility. Jesus said, in the second greatest command of all; *love your neighbor as **yourself**.* The Apostle Paul wrote to husbands, *So husbands ought to love their own wives as their own bodies; he who loves his wife* *loves himself.* (Eph. 5: 28) Such statements give clear indication that love of self is not a sin, placed in its proper context.

Mark this statement carefully: *A low esteem of self will result in low productivity*; thus **we need to gain a proper view, from God's perspective, of our own worth.**

WHAT IS MAN WORTH?

In The Eyes of God:

First, consider man's value **in the eyes of God**. Here is the real key in understanding what has been written. Consider the *value* that God the Father attached to man *before* the finished work of redemption. We are told in the eighth Psalm: one, God is concerned for and cares about man, as He said, *What is man that you are mindful of him, and the Son of Man that you visit him?* One recognizes this phrasing as a question, and yet it has exclamatory value as well: **What is man!**

Two, God gives man an exalted position, as I have suggested in the exclamation above, *What is man!* Substantiating this conclusion, read on: *For you [God] have made him a little lower than the angels, and have crowned him with glory and honor.* Yes! Glory and honor is God's design for man – in His purpose.

Three, Almighty God gave man great authority: *You [God] have made him to have dominion over the works of your hands; You [God] have put all things under his feet.*

Four, man is a creation and the work of God's hands, thus the greatness of His design: *All things were made through Him [Christ], and without Him [Christ] nothing was made that was made.* (John 1: 3). Again, God said, *Let us make man . . .* (Gen. 1: 26)

Expanding on these brief foundational comments, we summarize the truth as found in the creation account in Genesis, chapter one. God made man (v.26); gave him dominion over all the earth; and He saw that what He had made was **"very good"**! (Gen. 1: 31)

Now, looking forward to the New Testament, we see that God valued His created man enough that He gave *His only begotten son* to die sacrificially in redeeming him from eternal death. He valued man so highly that, in demonstrating His love for man, *while we were yet sinners, Christ died for us.* (Romans 5: 8)

How can all of this be true, in light of the earlier words regarding man in his sin? Man is marred by his rebellion, as we are told that *there is none righteous, none who does good – like sheep [that] have gone astray.*

How can the two views be reconciled? The answer: **God sees man for what he can be**, his potential when salvaged, and not for what he is.

I remember many years ago when a small boy, William Dedrick, brought a big, rough, ugly round rock to our house, and my wife, a lover and collector of rocks, immediately wanted it, and bargained for it. What could Jeanie possibly see in this rock, so as to want to possess it?

I couldn't see why she wanted that rock, so ugly on its exterior; but she saw beneath that rough exterior, *seeing what it could be.* She then had it cut and polished, revealing a beautiful geode of magnificent colors. Jean saw its potential: what it could be, and not what it was. Now it has been cut and made into beautiful book ends that have set on our book shelf for years.

Here is the way that our dear Father looks upon man, and why He values him so highly. He **values** him, not as a lowly sinner, but as one who was created in the image of Himself, crowned with *glory and honor,* capable of dominion over all the earth!

MAN'S VALUE AFTER RESTORATION

Now look at the value God attached to man *after* the finished work of redemption, when he is restored to his former high estate, one day to *be priests of God and of Christ, and shall reign with Him a thousand years.* (Rev. 20: 6) Those who have accepted God's master plan for their life are *heirs of God's, and joint heirs with Christ.* (Rom. 8: 17). They are called *heirs, children, sons, royal priesthood, fellow citizens, elect, saints,* in various references! Really, how far can we go?

He highly values those of you who are not yet saved, having paid the supreme price for your rescue. He gave His *only begotten*

Son for your redemption, buying you back from the slave market of sin. He sees you for what you can be, not for what you are.

Again, He highly values you who are saved, having great plans for you, having purchased you at so great a price, preparing you for a magnificent, eternal inheritance.

GET A NEW IMAGE OF YOURSELF

In Christ you *are not* a poor worm of the dust. Look at yourself as mirrored in God's image, as He sees you, as the Lord said to Samuel, *For the Lord does not see as man sees; for man looks at the outward appearance, but the Lord looks at the heart.* (I Samuel 16: 7)

Defeat the problems of life by enlarging the view of yourself. See yourself as He sees you; see your potential – what God wants to make of you.

HOW TO ENLARGE THE VIEW OF YOURSELF

From the outset, it is clear that this must be done, not from an egotistical self-sufficient fashion, but as the Bible admonishes: *Everyone who is among you [is] not to think of himself more highly than he ought to think, but to think soberly [humbly?] as God has dealt to each man a measure of faith.* (Romans 12: 3)

The enlarged view of self must be viewed in the frame in which God has placed him. Outside of God, in the framework of ego, outside of Christ, *Every man is altogether vanity.* The frame without God is empty.

To enlarge the view of yourself, what you are and what you can be, you must look through the eyes of God. The story is told, perhaps even apocryphal, of an artist painting a portrait of a beggar. When it was completed, the beggar asked, *Is it I? Can it be me?* The artist replied, *That is the man I see in you.* At that, the beggar replied, *If that's the man you see, that's the man I'll be!*

HOW TO SEE YOURSELF

You need to see yourself as God sees you:

He sees you as a distinct individual, made for a specific purpose, not like any other person or purpose, unique. Just as there are no two snowflakes exactly alike in their intricate, beautiful design, there are no two people exactly alike with exactly the same purpose, just as the DNA and fingerprint varies.

The truly exciting thing is that God designed you just as you are! The Psalmist said, *For You formed my inward parts, You covered me in my mother's womb. I will praise you, for I am fearfully and wonderfully made, marvelous are your works. And that my soul knows very well. My frame was not hidden from You, when I was made in secret, and skillfully wrought in the lowest parts of the earth. Your eyes saw my substance, being yet unformed, and in Your book they all were written, the days fashioned for me, when as yet there were none of them.* (Psalm 139: 13- 16)

He made me just as I am: a big proboscis, (as Cyrano de Bergerac would say, *A nose? Nay, a perch for birds. When I blow it, the Red Sea.* Maybe not quite that big, but still big). **Am I to be ashamed when** I look in the mirror? No, no, God made me this way, *fearfully and wonderfully*, and I must not despise God's creation.

So many Christians look at themselves, and because they are short, because they have thin lips, straight hair, big feet, large ears, they develop an inferiority that defeats them.

You need to remember that God made you as you are: *My frame was not hidden from you, when I was made in secret.* When you despise that and say, why do I look like this, you are questioning God, saying *God, you are a failure. You did a lousy job designing me.* Remember, He made you like you are for a purpose. To degrade yourself is to degrade God's work!

The attitude that wins is, *I will praise you: for I am fearfully and wonderfully made; marvelous are your works . . .* (Psalm 139: 14)

Your heavenly Father designed you as an individual, for a specific purpose; and if a handsome or beautiful face would get in the way of that purpose and distract from the glory of God, He alters the design.

Remember that Isaiah said about the Lord Jesus, *He has no form or comeliness; and when we see Him, there is no beauty that we should desire Him.* (Isaiah 53: 2). When you see an artist's conception of Jesus with a pretty face and beautiful flowing hair, which is not a likeness of my Savior, for He was designed for *who* He is and what He did, not for how He looked – made that way for that purpose!

Michelangelo once bought an inferior piece of marble, which no one would buy. Asked why he bought it, he said, *Because there is an angel in there and I must set it free.* Then he went to work with hammer and chisel, carving a magnificent statue of an angel.

DESIGNED FOR A PURPOSE

There may not be an angel inside, but there is something else designed for His glory and honor. Accept yourself and permit God to go to work and free that potential.

Moses had a speech impediment, causing him to plead, *oh, my Lord, I am not eloquent . . . . but I am slow of tongue.* (Exodus 4: 10). The Lord's answer revealed that it was He who had designed him. *So the Lord said to him, 'Who has made man's mouth? Or who makes the mute, the deaf, the seeing, or the blind? Have not I, the Lord? Now therefore, go, and I will be with your mouth and teach you what you shall say'.* (Exodus 4:11, 12)

Moses was made that way by the Creator, in order that God would be glorified and not Moses when Israel was liberated from Egyptian enslavement. Freedom was not won because of Moses' eloquence, but by God, in spite of Moses' stutter.

Jeremiah had a problem of a lack of self esteem for some reason, seemingly because of his youth, as he said *Ah, Lord God! Behold I cannot speak, for I am a child.* (Jer. 1: 7-9) Yet, God designed him for a purpose, and Jeremiah permitted God to free him for his designed purpose.

Paul had a thorn in the flesh, given to him by God, in order that that he could say of himself that he had an *infirmity of the flesh,* hideous enough that it could have caused people to despise and reject him. (Gal. 4:13, 14). Yet, he preached and taught in spite of it, which enhanced his ministry, as he said, *my strength is made perfect in weakness.* (2 Cor. 12: 19) God had designed Paul in that way in order to accomplish a specific purpose, in order that He would get the glory and not Paul.

Milton, who was blind, would write one of the world's great-est work, *Paradise Lost*; John Bunyan, in prison like the Apostle Paul, would write the world's greatest allegory, *Pilgrim's Progress;* Beethoven, composer of the immortal *Ninth Symphony,* was deaf.

All these, like pearls, produced great beauty from their affliction. Such is the work from God's hand. Permit Him to use any seem-ingly design flaw to work His glory through you!

For what purpose has God designed you? Do you know? You must see yourself as God sees you. On the other hand, to despise yourself in any way is to despise God's creation. *O man, who are you to reply against God? Will the thing formed say to Him who formed it, 'why have you made me like this'?* (Romans 9: 20)

You are *fearfully and wonderfully made . . . crowned with glory and honor.* See it; acknowledge it; say to the Father, *You made me as I am, my Master Designer; set my potential free.*

WHEN VICTORY OVER SELF COMES

As emphasized before, our Lord sees you for *what you can be.* Every person is essentially two persons: the one he is and the one only he can be. Victory will come when you can look at yourself, not in the light of present limitations, but at what you can become. This is what Paul was doing, as he wrote to the Philip-pians. *Brethren, I do not count myself to have apprehended; but one thing I do, forgetting those things which are behind and reaching forward to those things which are ahead, I press forward toward the goal for the prize of the upward call of God in Christ Jesus.* (Phil. 3: 13- 14)

Someone asked Thomas Edison how he accounted for his amazing inventive genius. He replied, *It is because I never think in words, I think in pictures.* He pictured in his mind what he wanted to invent, and the picture took possession of him, leading to a dedicated pursuit until his accomplishment measured up to the picture.

We need a picture of what we can be, permitting the Master Designer to work on us, tirelessly yielded to Him until the end is accomplished.

A successful writer of short stories said that he always wrote his stories backwards. First, he wrote the ending, and then he wrote the story to fit it. So, get in mind your highest potential, make it the goal of your life, working toward that potential. As Paul, *press toward the goal for the prize of the upward call of God in Christ Jesus.* (Phil. 3: 14)

How amazing it is to see how people live up to their expectations. One man told about a miserable, miserly woman who saved her money, but finally lost everything. She told him, *What I feared has come to pass. Here I am old and penniless. Now there is nothing but the poorhouse.* She feared poverty, expected poverty, pictured poverty, until it became a reality!

God sees you, and you should see yourself as *more than conquerors through Him [Jesus] who loved us,* over which not even *death nor life, nor angels, nor principalities nor powers, nor things present nor things to come, nor height nor depth, nor any other created thing, shall be able to separate us from the love of God which is in Christ Jesus our Lord.* (Romans 8:37- 39) – *who* gives us victory, making us *more than conquerors.*

Get that picture firmly fixed in your mind. See victory and not failure, as Paul said for himself, *I can do all things through Christ who strengthens me.* (Phil. 4: 13)

THIS TRUTH ASSURED

You may say, I've done these things and my life doesn't look very victorious. Remember two things: one, God is not finished with you yet. Such is the truth expressed by the Apostle Paul to the Ephesians, *For we are His workmanship, created in Christ Jesus for good works. . . ;* and that work is a project in process.

I remember learning to emphasize this truth many years ago while attending Bill Gothard's Basic Youth Conflict seminar in Oakland, California. Bill had us memorize these letters, *"PBPGINFWMY,"* meaning, *Please be patient, God is not finished with me yet.*

Two, what seems to be a failure to you may simply be classed a failure in worldly standards, but need not be in the eyes of God.

I pictured myself as preaching to thousands, but never reached over maybe 350 or 400 in my one 28 year pastorate. Had I failed? God led me into ministering to many churches later in an interim pastoral ministry, and a combination of all of the numbers in those churches measured up to what I had dreamed! The goal was just attained in a different way!

Mozart went to Vienna at the age of 25, dying 10 years later. He composed music over those years which will live as long as people appreciate good music. Ironically, at one point, his publisher said to him harshly, *Write, sir, in a more easy and popular style; or I will neither print your music nor pay a penny for it.*

Mozart and his wife were so poor they often had neither food nor fuel. One morning, while so impoverished, a friend found them even waltzing to keep warm, all while he could have sacrificed his standards; but he kept his faith and fulfilled his potential, although it cost him his life in 10 years. We may have never heard of him if he had compromised his chosen destiny!

We have pictured Paul the Apostle of Christ, who persisted in spite of a hideous *thorn in the flesh,* so hideous that he complimented the Galatians for their willingness to hear him, in spite of his appearance. His persistence would result in the record of a major portion of the New Testament. John Whyte, eloquent Scottish preacher, scholar and saint, would persist in spite of his illegitimate birth. The students of Bishop Lightfoot said of this great scholar of the scriptures, *he was startlingly ugly {having} grotesque features and a squint,* yet he persisted, fulfilling God's marvelous plan for his life.

You may seem to be failing in the eyes of the world, but remember, look at what you can be through the Creator's eyes, not lowering your standards to get along. Remember, He isn't finished working with you yet, and will never finish 'til glorification!

As God said to King Jehoshaphat, *The battle is not yours, but God's.* (II Chronicles 20: 15)

CHAPTER FOUR

STUDY AND DISCUSSION GUIDE

Note: There are three study and discussion guides for chapter four.

Lesson One:

1. Is it proper for a Christian to say, *I'm no good, extolling perceived weakness?* (Romans 3:10- 12)
   Discuss your answer

2. What is the author's goal for you in this chapter?

3. Is it proper for man to love himself? (Eph. 5: 28, Mat. 9: 19)

4. The author said, *A low esteem of yourself will result in low* _____. Fill in the blank and discuss the validity of the statement.

5. What is the true worth of man? (Psalm 8: 4; Job 7: 17).

6. Consider a second meaning other than a question in Psalm 8: 4.

7. How highly has God valued man? (Genesis 1: 31; John 3: 16; Romans 5: 8)

8. How does God see man? For what he is or _____ _____ _____ _____. Discuss the example of William Dedrick's rock and its application.

Lesson Two

1. In getting a new image of yourself, see how God views you. (I Samuel 19: 7)

2. Name a caution to be exercised when you view yourself. (Romans 12: 3) Discuss.

3. What is the moral of the story of the artist painting a portrait of a beggar?

4. Does God view you as an individual, and if so, how? (Psalm 139:13- 16) Discuss.

5. Focus on verse 14 of the above reference and discuss.

6. Explain how one can value God's design in the face of distorted or unattractive features. What happens if you blame God for such a condition?

7. Why was Moses made the way he was? (Exodus 4:11- 12)

8. Explain the value of Paul's thorn in the flesh. (II Cor. 12: 9, Gal. 4:13, 14)

Lesson Three

1. There are essentially two persons when considering self. Name them and discuss.

2. How does Paul deal with the above question? (Phil. 3:13- 14)

3. How did Thomas Edison explain why he had such inventive genius? Discuss and apply lesson.

4. Consider Romans 8:37- 39 in describing how you should see yourself.

5. Is there ever a time in your life when you are all you can be, and all that God intends you to be? (Ephesians 2: 10).

6. Discuss the lesson taken from the example of Mozart.

7. When will God truly be finished with you? (Rom. 8:28- 30)

8. What did God tell Jehoshaphat in II Chron. 20: 15? How does that apply to this lesson?

CHAPTER FIVE

SPIRITUAL ENEMY #1: THE FLESH

VICTORY THROUGH FAITH

As we considered the steps to a victorious life in previous chapters, we considered four steps as suggested in the letter to the Romans, chapter six. They were:

- *Know* what Christ has already done for you;
- *Trust* Him to make that a finished fact in your life;
- *Yield* every area of your life to the Lordship of Christ; and
- *Obey* in service.

We made application of these four steps, considering them in the hands of the Potter, knowing what He has already provided as we place the clay [self] in the Potter's hands; *yielding* every part to Him for molding, *obeying* by placing the vessel into His hand for use.

Sounds simple enough when stated that way, but *how to* take each step may seem overwhelming. I am reminded of a Marine Captain who had just completed a 50 mile forced march with his company. The Captain halted the men in front of the company barracks, elated at their outstanding accomplishment, he announced: *Men, we're going to repeat this hike. Any man who thinks he cannot make it, step forward two paces.* The entire company, with the exception of one Private, stepped forward. The Captain was shaken, but he recovered in time to congratulate the single volunteer for having the courage to be willing to hike another 50 miles.

Walk another 50 miles? mumbled the dazed Private, *Sir, I can't even take 2 steps forward!*

Another illustration regarding this problem: a Petty Officer at recruit training singled out a recruit and gave him orders, *Take this bicycle and deliver this message,* handing him the message. The officer added, *and hustle right back.* The recruit was expected to return in about 5 minutes, but half an hour later he finally came into view, slowly pushing the bike. *What happened?* asked the exasperated officer. *You have a flat tire or something? No,* replied the recruit, *I just don't know how to ride a bicycle!*

You may have been trying to flesh out what to do in taking the aforementioned steps, but don't know how, like the recruit with the bicycle. Your answer *how* comes, in the main, in the letter to the Galatians, chapter three, verses one through eleven, where we are told, in part, *The just shall live by faith.* These instructions being the key, we will consider how you, personally, can implement the faith life, learning how to be victorious over the flesh by faith.

THE JUST SHALL LIVE BY FAITH

Real light is available in Galatians, chapter three on how the just can live by faith.

Suppose we begin by simply reading the first three verses: *O foolish Galatians! Who has bewitched you that you should not obey the truth, before whose eyes Jesus Christ was clearly portrayed among you as crucified? This only I want to learn from you. Did you receive the Spirit by the works of the law, or by the hearing of faith? Are you so foolish? Having begun in the Spirit, are you now being made perfect by the flesh?* (Galatians 3: 1-3)

I ordinarily discourage even looking at the so called *Living Bible,* but make an exception this one time:

> *Then have you gone completely crazy? For*
> *if trying to obey the Jewish laws never gave*
> *you Spiritual life in the first place, why do you*
> *think that trying to obey them now will make you*
> *stronger Christians? (Galatians 3: 3)*

The Galatians were foolishly inconsistent; they had come to Christ by faith, had been saved; and had received the Holy Spirit, and now were trying to live under the law. They were on a *flesh trip,* endeavoring to live the Christian life *in the flesh.*

As a result, the inspired apostle gave them their solution, and ours. *The just shall live by faith* – period. Yet, suppose we break that power-packed little statement of 6 words apart for understanding.

DEFINING FAITH

Our first question: **What is faith?** I am convinced that more Christians fail in living the faith life because they do not know what faith is, more than any other reason, thinking that faith is something to be *worked up* in the flesh, often substituting feeling for faith, mistaking the two.

What is faith? The only definition given in the scriptures is found in Hebrews, chapter eleven, verse 1: *Now faith is the substance of things hoped for, the evidence of things not seen.*

First, *faith is* **substance**, the actual realization of things for which you have hoped.

Second, *faith is* **evidence**, the proof or confidence of things you have not seen. Faith is taking God's word as proof, although you have not tasted, touched, or seen by the flesh.

Those two comments give a short, basic definition, but even then may be difficult to understand. Before moving on from the Hebrew's definition, note that little word *is.* Faith *is* evidence; faith **is** substance. Faith **is** the only evidence one will ever need regarding the promises of God! Faith is substance, turning promises from God into reality.

Hebrews eleven, verse six will help in understanding. *But without faith it is impossible to please Him [God] for he who comes to God must believe that He **is** and that He **is** a rewarder of those who diligently seek Him.*

Here, then, are the two facets of Biblical faith: one, believe that He is, that is, that God really exists as Creator, ruler, sustainer of the universe, and the Savior of man; and two, *believe that He is a rewarder of them who diligently seek Him,* that is, believe His word, believe that He will do what He says He will do: provide for your every need and care for you in both time and eternity.

Permit me to illustrate crudely but understandably what is meant. Suppose the car dealer says when you go to buy a car, *You can put your faith in this car.* What he means is: one, you can believe that *it is* what he says *it is:* a new, powerful, comfortable automobile; and two, that it *will do* what he says it *will do*: go 100 mph, get 30 miles per gallon of gasoline, run 100,000 miles without repair.

Now, I'm not pretending to compare God to a car dealer, heaven forbid, but am illustrating simple truth. As you ostensibly take the car dealer's word, by faith, you take God's word in the same two areas; One, that He is who He says He is, and Two, He will do what He says He will do.

Faith is not a thing. Faith is not a feeling. Faith is believing God's word and acting on it! As James writes, *Faith without works is dead* – no faith at all. Furthermore, he adds, *I will show you my faith by my works.* (James 2: 20, 18)

THE SOURCE OF FAITH

The next question is: **What is faith's source?** Where can you get it? God gives it to you. Amazing, God gives faith, and God receives faith. We read the answer in the following verse, *So then faith comes by hearing, and hearing by the word of God.* (Romans 10: 17) *God, by His trustworthiness,* **gives us the ability** *to believe.*

I have heard people say: I have no faith, and am simply incapable of faith. What so many lose sight of is that we live by faith daily. We have faith in the packager and the preserver of foods when he says that the contents of the package are as specified, and that they have included nothing injurious to health. We have faith in the cook who prepares the food, depending on him that he has not used pork with trichinosis, or a food with botulism, or ptomaine. We have faith in the auto maker that he has not put inferior materials in his product that will endanger our lives. We have faith in the pilot who flies the airplane, the bus driver who drives the bus. There is *nothing* we do that does not include at least a measure of faith, and when we do it, we do not feel as though we have done a remarkable thing!

My late wife Jean and I, along with my daughter Janet and our friend Naomi were touring in Switzerland several years ago. One day we were travelling to one of the great mountain peaks in the Swiss Alps, riding in a metal box with windows and doors, running on what appeared to be a steel cable. As I recall we were crossing an abyss at 5,000 feet. The four of us, along with a car load of people, did not have the slightest idea about exactly how that car operated. Was the car moving on the cable; or was the cable moving? Just how did that car climb that steep grade with such a heavy load?

The point was that we did not know, nor did we care. We rested by faith in the great skills of the Swiss, being demonstrated everywhere we travelled. Our only care was to arrive at the promised destination, so as to be thrilled by the dazzling vista we would behold. Such should be the case in our journey with God, trusting Him to bring us safely to that glorious vista that He promises. Because of faith, we had no fear in being suspended 5,000 feet in the air!

I thought about my flight here to Maui, where I am today as I edit this manuscript. For five hours I was suspended in an aircraft tens of thousands of feet above the earth. I really don't need to be precise about the height, for what's the difference in ten or twenty thousand feet at this height? I was told there was a pilot flying the aircraft, but I had never seen him! How did I know that he was behind that closed door about a hundred feet in front of me? How did I know that metal contraption could stay up there with all of those people?

You might answer, *Glennon, it's just a matter of aerodynamics! Aero what!!* I don't even know what the word means! Well then, wasn't I jumping out of my skin with worry, with not even a parachute? Actually I was reading a novel, and at other times trying to sleep. How could I do that? How? By faith, faith that there was a pilot behind that door; faith in Boeing Aircraft Corporation and their product. . . . .

We trust man, his products, his works, and provisions as though we have done nothing, without a thought, but let someone trust God and it becomes a miraculous feat. It is high time for us to realize, as Jesus said, *If you then, being evil, know how to give good gifts to your children, how much more will your Father who is in heaven give good things to those who ask Him.* (Matthew 7: 11).

One needs to realize what he is saying when he says, *I have no faith.* What he is really saying is *I have no faith in God. I cannot believe God.*

Faith does not depend on you; Faith depends on the trustworthiness of God!

If I say that I have faith in you, this is a tribute to you and your dependability, and not to me. If I say that I can depend on my pastor to preach God's Word, this is a tribute to him and not to me.

One who says that he has no faith in God is saying that he has not found God to be trustworthy. He can trust God for holding the universe together; and does not run about with *Chicken Little* crying that the earth is falling; but at the same time cannot trust God for his own puny self!

Faith comes from God, based on His trustworthiness.

DEPEND ON FAITH, NOT FLESH

The key statement that we have been repeating, *The just shall live by faith,* appears three times in the Scriptures, with the exact wording (with one small exception). (Habakkuk 2: 4, Galatians 3: 11, and Romans 1: 17).

A different emphasis is indicated in each of these three references:

THE JUST

The emphasis is on **the just** in Romans 1:17; with the emphasis that *justification*, being justified, made just, depends on faith. Man cannot be rightly related to God in any other way. The Bible says, *Therefore, having been **justified by faith**, we have peace with God through our Lord Jesus Christ.* (Romans 5: 1)

Again, we read in Ephesians 2:8, 9: *For by grace you have been **saved through faith**, and that not of yourselves; it is the gift of God.* Faith, not flesh works, brings a right relationship with the Father. Going back to our reference in Galatians, we are told, *Just as Abraham believed God, and it was accounted to him for right-eousness.* (Galatians 3: 6). Remember the reference to the faith of Abraham in the letter to the Hebrews: *By faith Abraham obeyed God when . . . he went out, not knowing where he was going.*

He *went out* because of faith, not to produce faith. God declared Abraham righteous, not because of all of his works, but on the basis of his faith. *For what does the Scripture say? Abraham believed God [faith] and it was accounted to him for righteousness.* (Romans 4: 3)

What a great faith! Where did he get it? How was such faith possible? It was founded on the trustworthiness of God. Listen to the exchange between young Isaac and his father Abraham, just as Abraham was about to sacrifice Isaac as an offering:

> *But Isaac spoke to Abraham . . . and he said, 'Look, the fire and the wood, but where is the lamb for the sacrifice?' And Abraham said, 'My son, God will provide for Himself the lamb for a burnt offering.'* (Genesis 22: 7, 8)

God will provide, said Abraham, and God did provide. You see again, Abraham's faith was based on the trustworthiness of God; and by faith he was accounted just.

The Just shall live by faith. Are you counted among the just because of your faith? God has provided a Lamb, as the Bible declares concerning the Lord Jesus Christ, *Behold the Lamb of God who takes away the sin of the world.* (John 1: 29)

By such a provision, He proves Himself to be absolutely trust-worthy, a wonderful basis for your faith. You do not have to work up faith within yourself. He provided the basis in this wonderful, all sufficient sacrifice. Would you like to be counted among the just? Then believe God; accept the trustworthiness of what He has already done for you. Why not do it right now? Bow with me and pray this prayer of faith, a faith that ever defeats the flesh!

> *Father, I accept the sacrifice of your Son as being sufficient to pay for my sin; take away my guilt, and make me just. I trust Jesus as my Savior, and call upon Him right now to save me. Amen.*

The Bible says: *Whosoever shall call upon the name of the Lord shall be saved.* (Romans 10: 13) Believe God that *He is a rewarder of them who diligently seek Him,* and that He will do exactly as He promises.

The Just – *shall live by faith.*

SHALL LIVE

In the second context, the emphasis is on **shall live.** *The Just* **SHALL LIVE** *by faith.*

> *But that no one is justified by the law in the sight God is evident, for 'the just **shall live** by faith.*
> *(Galatians 3: 11)*

We are rightly related to God on the basis of faith, and we maintain that relationship in the same fashion. God's good favor came by faith, and continues as one *lives* by faith. As Paul would ask the foolish Galatians, *Are you so foolish? Having begun in the spirit, are you now being made perfect by the flesh?* (Galatians 3: 3) The obvious answer to his question is a resounding *no!* However, this does not mean that there should not be works. Quite to the contrary, there will be works if there is genuine faith and life. Like Abraham's, they will result from faith and not the flesh. James makes it absolutely clear that true faith *shall live* and will result in works, but those works are of the spirit and not the flesh. *Shall live by faith* is just like having faith; it is a life built on the belief that God *is* and that He is a *rewarder* of them who diligently seek Him. It is a belief that *God* is present (Psalm 46: 1), and that He will never leave or forsake us (Hebrews 13: 5). It is the belief that what He says is true, with the quiet, confident, acceptance that *all things [do] work together for the good to those who love God, to those who are called according to His purpose.* (Romans 8: 28) And that we can, as the Bible says, *In everything give thanks, for this is the will of God in Christ Jesus for you.* (I Thessalonians 5: 18)

If I yield myself into His hands, faith accepts the life just as He dispenses, without rebellion.

A good friend leaves the church I pastor for no apparent reason, as numbers do, when they are still desperately needed. Why? The wound is severe. Pain shrouds the heart like the darkness of despair. Then I am reminded that God has a purpose, as He works in refining my life and the life of the church. Faith then says, *Thank you Father,* for I trust your will and plan.

Oh, it hurts like the ingrown toe-nail in a too-tight shoe, pulsing with every beat of the heart, but I know that my heavenly Father is at work in my life and that of the church. Some unseen thing is being accomplished, about which I may know nothing, but faith enables me to say thanks and trust in my trustworthy heavenly Father.

Now, you cannot say in the face of that: Glennon Culwell is a real man of faith. No, that action is not predicated on Glennon Culwell, but on God's trustworthiness. It is He who made the promise and keeps it. Anything less on my part would be rank unbelief!

Faith in God's faithful provisions makes all things possible. Young Joseph was forced to endure a period in the dungeon, and in slavery, before it was God's timing for him to be Governor over all of Egypt. Abraham went through many trying years, and trials, in becoming the right leader to found God's nation. Abraham Lincoln waited through years of frustrating experiences, facing one failure after another, before he was seasoned for the service he would give to his country. **The point: God always knows best how to direct your life, in accomplishing His purpose.**

The poet *Coleridge* captured the emphasis that faith *lives, or acts,* in these words:

> *Think not the faith by which the just shall live*
> *Is a dead creed, a map correct of heaven . . .*
> *It is an affirmation and an act*
> *That bids eternal truth be present fact.*
> *"The just **SHALL LIVE** by faith."*

BY FAITH

In the third context, the emphasis is on *by faith.* Actually Habakkuk 2: 4 says, *The just shall live by **his faith**. Behold the proud* [who trusts in his flesh]. *His soul is not upright in him* [he is as phony as the proverbial three dollar bill]; *but the just* [the genuine, real McCoy] *shall live **by his faith***.

The Christian life is a faith life, as the inspired writer to the Hebrews writes, *but without faith it is impossible to please God.* Shocking are the words of the Apostle Paul as he writes, *Whatever is not from faith is sin.* (Romans 14: 23)

One's efforts in the flesh constitute mistrust of God. The idea that God won't bless you, if you don't cook up some good works in your own ability, is like saying that you must earn the grace of God, the very antithesis of the meaning of grace. *Therefore it is of faith that it might be according to grace . . .* (Romans 4: 16)

*The just shall live **by his faith**.*

WILL TO LIVE BY FAITH

You begin by the exercise of *your will*, your committed desire. *If any man **will** come after me, Jesus said, let him deny himself, take up his cross, and follow me.* (Matthew 16: 24)

Man is spirit, soul, and body. The soul is composed of intellect [mind], emotions, and will. This is the *ego*, self, which causes so much trouble in its rebellion against God. Here is the reason Jesus said, *let him deny himself.* Self is to exercise its will to give itself over to Him. *If any man **wills** to do his will . . .* (John 7: 17) There it is: we are to will to do His will, that is, give Him the rule over your life; determine to make Christ King.

I am reminded here of a delightful story told by the late Bill Bright, founder of Campus Crusade for Christ. I've personally heard Bill relate this story, and have heard it countless times as he lectured about the Spirit-filled life.

He told about how his small son Brad refused to eat his breakfast one morning. Vonette, Bill's wife, had fixed *egg in a bonnet*, placing the egg in the hole in the middle of a piece of toast. Bill said, *Brad, eat your breakfast.* Brad replied, *I don't want it.* After a continuing exchange and a few tears, Dr. Bright found the key. He asked, *Brad, who is on the throne of your life this morning?* With this the tears really began to flow. Brad had learned the concept that Christ was to be on the throne of his life. So the small boy replied, *The devil and me.* Dr. Bright then asked, *Who do you **want** it to be?* Brad answered, *Jesus.* Whereupon Bill said let's pray, with Brad praying, *Dear Jesus, forgive me for being disobedient, and help me to like this egg.* God heard his prayer and he enjoyed his breakfast. That evening Dr. Bright asked his small son, *Brad, who has been on the throne of your life today?* He replied, *Jesus. Oh,* he added, *except at breakfast this morning.*

When you will to do His will, make him king and permit Him to reign; He makes the *'eggs of life'* palatable. Here is what is meant when we are told, **Yield** *yourselves to God . . .* (Romans 6: 13, KJV). The NKJV says, *present yourself to God...* - will to live by faith. Give yourselves to the Lord. Say to Him, *Your will be done in my life!*

The late Dr. B. H. Carroll of Southwest Baptist Theological Seminary fame, where I attended seminary, had been an avowed atheist, and was converted by the influence of this promise, *If any man **will to do His will,** he shall know the doctrine, whether it be of God or whether I speak of myself.* (John 7: 17). Carroll was 23 years old when he returned from the Civil War. The war had broken his body; His sin of disbelief had broken his spirit. While riding down a country road one day, he came to a brush arbor where a revival meeting was in progress. The Spirit of God drew Carroll toward the service, arriving just in time to hear the preacher extend an invitation to the lost to be saved, quoting this very verse of scripture.

With all of his heart, the young man wanted to know the truth. Responding to the invitation, people began to shout. Harvey Carroll, the atheist, was professing his faith in Christ. Standing at the altar, tottering on his cane, he stilled the congregation, explaining to them that he was only committing himself to the proposition that, if a man *will to do His will, he shall know.* With that first upward reach toward God, the sin-tossed young man found God reaching down to him. That night, while alone in his room, B. H. Carroll, founder of Southwestern Baptist Theological Seminary became a child of God's by faith, receiving Christ as his personal Savior.

The starting place of the faith life is the exercise of your will to do so, a simple decision and determination.

Will to live by faith!

HE ACCEPTS YOUR COMMITMENT

How can one know whether the Lord accepts your commitment to grant Him the throne of your life?

We have already found that it isn't by works, or by feeling. Too many fall short at this point, for a lack of emotional feelings.

I introduce people to the Savior, ask them how they know He entered their lives, and more often than not the reply is, I *feel* different or . . . I *think. . . .* I'm reminded of a friend I introduced to Christ as Savior. I asked how he knew Christ came into his life. In response he said that he felt peace. Wonderful, but my emphasis to him and others is that emotional feelings cannot be trusted.

We will to do His will; give ourselves to God; yield to Him; present ourselves to Him; and then, if feelings don't come, we sense failure. The emotions clamor for dominance like a harpy-fish-wife, but God says, *The just shall live by faith.* If you will to know, you will know on the basis of faith.

The proper order is: fact, faith, and then possibly feelings, *and* you are in trouble when you try to reverse that order. When God says, *My son, give me your heart,* the FACT is present that He will take it when proffered. Next, we accept by FAITH that He did accept it. Then FEELINGS may come, but failure to feel emotionally is never a factor in determining the validity of one's exercise of will!

Now, don't get me wrong. Thank God for feelings. Don't suppress them. Yet, don't permit them to dominate, or the lack of them to cast doubt. Bob Harrington said he was so high the night that he received Christ that he passed *the flying nun* on his way home!

Wonderful, but his conversion would have been no less real without the feeling. The Christian is far out of bounds when he seeks an emotional experience or feeling to validate faith! Depend on feelings, and when the emotions run dry, as they invariably do, despair and confusion result.

How can you know He accepts your will? The Leviticus law of offerings to the Lord provides the answer. Everything given to Him becomes, by that very act, something holy, and something that cannot, without sacrilege, be put to any other use. The Bible says, *Nevertheless no devoted offering that a man may devote to the Lord of all that he has, both man and beast, or the field of his possession, shall be sold or redeemed; every devoted offering is most holy to the Lord.* (Leviticus 27: 28)

That gift does not become invalid just because of a lack of feelings. You gave; God accepts. When He says *Present your bodies a living sacrifice, holy, acceptable unto God . . .* (Romans 12: 1), the commitment is there to receive your sacrifice. Demanding a feeling from God, to validate that offering, is an insult to Him, making a mockery of faith. And when you take it back and use it for something else, because of a lack of feeling, sacrilege results.

When you truly yield yourself to God, to live the faith life, He accepts the offering!

The husband keeps asking his wife, *Do you love me? Do you love me? Do you love me?* And that doubt makes for an uncertain, unfulfilling relationship. You nag God; *Am I yours? Did you accept me? How do I know? Give me some kind of feeling;* and that wavering attitude produces a wavering, defeated life.

Make His will supreme by simply giving Him your will; give Him rule over your life; as Brad Bright, put Him on the throne of your life; accept it as an accomplished fact. Believe that He will do what He promises.

APPLICATION

The just shall live by faith. Believe that He is, and that He is a rewarder of them who diligently seek Him. Then *will* to live the faith life, and follow it to victory. ***Victory through Faith!***

By faith Abel . . .; by faith Noah . . .; by faith Abraham . . .; by faith Jacob . . .; by faith Joseph . . .; by faith Moses . . .; by faith Rahab . . . (Hebrews 11) These great men and women of God operated by faith. My prayer is that, *by faith*, you would enter into the victorious Christian life!

The three women, Mary Magdalene, Mary the mother of James, and Salome, did not turn back in despair, while knowing that they did not have the strength to remove the stone from the door of Jesus' tomb. Even though they knew the task was beyond their power, they went forward in faith, and God rolled away the stone!

There will be stones in your path. If you *will* go forward in faith, God will remove the stones that need to be removed, opening your path to the victorious abundant life.

Put Jesus on the throne!

CHAPTER FIVE

STUDY AND DISCUSSION GUIDE

1. Review and name the four steps to the victorious Christian life. (Romans 6). Discuss the meaning of each one.

2. How can you take those steps? Consider the two steps you can choose to take. Which one is the only way? Habakkuk 2: 4; Galatians 3: 11; Romans 1: 17.

3. Explain the definition of faith as found in Hebrews 11: 1.

4. What is the source of faith? Romans 12: 3; Matthew 7: 11. Faith depends on the _____ of God. Discuss.

5. Explain and discuss the three-fold divisions of Romans 1: 17 *("The Just"); Galatians 3: 11 ("Shall live"),* Habakkuk 2: 14 *("By his faith")*

6. How does one begin the faith life? Matthew 16: 24; John 7: 17; Romans 10: 17. Discuss.

7. Tell and discuss the exchange between Dr. Bill Bright and his son Brad.

8. Are feelings dependable? If not, on what do we depend?

9. Is Christ on the throne of your life? How do you put Him there?

CHAPTER SIX

SPIRITUAL ENEMY #2: DOUBT

DEFEATING THE PROBLEMS OFF LIFE

*. . .he who doubts is like a wave of the
sea driven and tossed by the wind. . .
He is a double-minded man, unstable in all his ways. (James 1: 6b, 8)*

The Federal Bureau of Investigation developed a list they called the *10 Most Wanted*, focusing on the most wanted criminals at large, giving each one a priority designation of one through ten, with *Public Enemy Number One* at the top.

We have followed their practice by developing a list of *Spiritual Enemies* to the Christian life. The author arbitrarily labeled *flesh,* a wide-encompassing term, as Private Enemy #1.

I wonder if you would not agree with me that next on our list should be *doubt, Private Enemy #2.* Is there anything other than the flesh itself that defeats the faith–life more than doubt, a varying measure of unbelief? Doubt is as foreign to faith as Mother Teresa to strip poker!

We have emphasized that, to arrest and defeat the flesh, *The just are to live by faith.* Doubt, unbelief, the very opposite of faith, must then be of major concern. The admonition of the Savior gives us a proper beginning for this consideration, as He admonishes Thomas, *Do not be unbelieving, but believing.* (John 20: 27) or as the King James phrases it,

*Be not **faithless** but believing.*

61

The words, which are good advice for Thomas the doubter, are good for you and me, if we are to *arrest* and defeat this enemy of our soul!

DOUBT DEFINED

The word *apistia* in the Greek original, translated *unbelief,* carries the connotation of *distrust, lack of faith,* or really just plain unbelief. That Greek word is a combination of the word *pistis*, meaning *faith* or *belief,* with *"a" or alpha* placed at its beginning, making it mean *no faith,* or *no belief.* For example, we do that in the English language with such a word as *moral,* and by adding an *"a"*, thus it becomes *amoral meaning no morals.* A *theist* believes in a God, an *atheist believes in no God* – unbelief in another form.

So, how can one attribute *apistia* or *unbelief* to a *believer,* a seeming paradox? Perhaps we can explain the answer like this: He believes in God, in Christ as his Savior, but at times he distrusts God, not believing that He either can or will do a certain thing for him; we call that doubt. On the other hand, a believer may question something about the reality or personality of the Lord, an act of *apistia* or *doubt.*

Take Matthew 17 as an example, where the disciples could not cast the demon out of a small child. Why not? Because, as Jesus said they were faithless - *apistia. O faithless and perverse generation . . .* Jesus addressed them. (Matthew 17: 17). They believed in Jesus, but didn't believe that He could or would do what He had said He would through them.

Perhaps a consideration of Matthew 10: 1 will help our understanding. *And when He [Jesus] had called His twelve disciples to Him, He gave them power over unclean spirits, to cast them out . . . .* (Matthew 10: 1). Though He had given them power to cast out demons, and they believed *in* Him, yet they were unbelieving regarding the power He had given to them! Sounds like doubletalk, and that's the mess doubt produces!

He had said to them, *I give you power to cast out unclean spirits [demons] . . .* They would say *Wonderful, here we go.* Then what happened, when they were faced with an actual case of demon possession? They began to bite their nails and say, *Did the Master really mean we could cast out demons, in a case like this?* You see, things changed when they were confronted by an actual case. Perhaps, then, they said half-heartedly, *Come out, doubting* that the demon would really come out of the child. What happened? The child's father said, *They could not cure him.* (Matthew 17: 16) Doubt leads to defeat, or failure!

That's what *doubt* does to a man of faith; it cancels his faith out when it comes to application in real life situations. No wonder we label it *Spiritual Enemy #2!*

So, when we speak of doubt, we speak of it in the sense of *unbelief* or *distrust.*

Here is a homely little example from my far distant past, an event that I recorded. I was wearing a pair of pants, in which the entire bottom of the right front pocket was worn out. As a result, I put my change, knife, and keys in the left pocket, thinking it trust-worthy. I was standing listening to Ken Poure speak to a group of ladies in our church, when a coin dropped down my pants leg to the floor. I reached down and picked it up, thinking as I did, *uh-oh, I can't trust that pocket either.* So I switched everything out, putting it in my coat pocket. I didn't trust that pocket *(apistia)*; I no longer believed in it!

Wait a minute! There is a second word in the Greek translated *doubt,* and that is the word *diakrino.* This word literally means, *to separate, discriminate,* or *to judge.* Thus, when it is translated *doubt,* it means *to be divided in one's mind*, or simply means *indeci-sion.* A divided mind, indecision, is unstable and faithless.

A perfect illustration of this meaning is found where Jesus speaks of commanding a mountain to be removed into the sea. He says a person can do that if he *shall not doubt (diakrino) in his heart, but shall believe . . . .* How many of you have tried to cast mountains into the sea: mountains of worry, guilt, bitterness, and they have not gone? You then say, *I knew it wouldn't work; You really can't cast mountains into the sea.*

Is this conclusion really accurate? How many of you have ever approached this question with a truly undivided mind, and actually tried? I don't know anyone who has tried it, really believing that he or she could actually cast a mountain into the sea! The promise ever waits for one of that strong a faith!

The problem is really *diakrino*, a divided mind, indecision. You say, *Mountain, be cast into the sea, while saying to yourself, I knew it wouldn't work – doubt, unbelief, a divided mind.*

You protest, why don't you try a simpler task than casting mountains? Because that one works every time! I've tried it, but never believed I could do it! Skeptics point to that promise, trying to dispute the validity of the Lord's promises. There's nothing wrong with the promise, no one has ever tried it with that kind of faith! Think you can?

A third word translated *doubt* is the Greek word *distazo*, meaning literally, *to hesitate, to stand divided, to doubt.* You conclude, isn't that what doubt does? It hesitates, and as the old proverb says, *He who hesitates is lost.*

Hesitation, doubt *(distazo)* sacrifices the blessings of God! What Biblical example leaps into your mind? Mine turns to the time Peter tried to walk on the water, just to begin sinking. Remember the story? Jesus came walking out across the water toward the boat that held Peter and other disciples. Peter said, *Lord, if it is you...* Hold it right there. Hadn't they just said it was *a ghost,* when they first saw Him? Here was Peter's first doubt; but that being settled, he went ahead to say, *Lord, if it is you (and it is), command me to come to you on the water. Let me walk on the water, too.* The Master replied, *come,* and when Peter stepped out of the boat, it was like his feet hit pavement. Can't you hear him saying to the others, *Just look at me. I'm walking on the water.* About that time he looked up and saw the stormy seas, realized where he was, and you know the rest of the story. Jesus had to catch him, saying to Peter, *O you of little faith, why did you doubt, why did you hesitate distazo)?* Hesitation would have drowned him had Jesus not lifted him up. (Matthew 14: 25-31)

Little faith put Peter on the water, but *hesitation* sank him. When he hesitated (doubted), he took his eyes off of Jesus and put them on the storm.

God promises, *Casting all your care upon Him, for He cares for you.* (I Peter 5: 7). So you give care a heave, *Here, Lord, you take it.* Then you hesitate, reach out to take it back, thinking, *will He really bear it? After all, doesn't God help those who help themselves? He expects me to take care of my own problems.*

Here we find a good description of how we really rationalize our own trust in our heavenly Father. We doubt God's promises all the time, and almost sink under the weight of those cares which He seeks to bear!

APPLICATION

There are still other words translated *unbelief* and *doubt,* but you should have the picture by now.

No wonder so few Christians fail to defeat the flesh, put it to death by faith, *'reckon'* it so, and then live a defeated Christian life.

They *apistia,* they doubt; they just don't believe God when He makes such promises as this: *You [God] will keep him in perfect peace, whose mind is stayed on you, because he trusts in you. Trust in the Lord forever, for in YAH, the lord is everlasting strength.* (Isaiah 26: 3-4)

How many really believe that? Trust will bring perfect peace, because of the everlasting strength of Yahweh? Few really manifest that kind of peace, contentment with the Lord and His provisions. Why? Because of unbelief. They no more believe in that kind of peace than they believe they can cast a mountain into the sea.

Others are defeated by *diakrino,* they have *divided minds.* A young man said to me, *I want to get right with God. I've been living two different lives;* and they were tearing him apart. He believed God, but he didn't believe God. How can such a statement be true? *Diakrino, a divided mind.*

Then others are defeated by *distazo,* uncertainty, hesitancy, doubt. Jesus said, *Come to me, all you who labor and are heavy laden, and I will give you rest.* (Matthew 11: 28). Many respond, give me rest, Lord. I really need it, but then they *distazo, hesitate,* remaining burdened with care, defeated.

You must make up your mind. Is God really trustworthy? Can you really trust His Word?

I woke up one morning recently and it suddenly dawned on me, I'm 85 years old today. God has been so good to me, giving me all of those years, 85 of them, filled with His blessings and most of all, a life filled with purpose for 60 of those 85 years. I may not have total *perfect peace*, but my Father is faithfully at work daily perfecting it; I may face times of indecision, but my Savior is constantly faithfully calling, *follow me*, and as I do I find rest; I may lose direction for a moment, but I find my way is His way, as He says, *here is the way, walk in it*.

Perfect peace, rest, an abundant life, and then: *As for me, I will see your face in righteousness; I shall be satisfied when I awake in Your likeness.* (Psalm 17: 15)

My Father is trustworthy. What a God! What a Savior! I need only heed His admonition, *Be not faithless, but believing;* and answer as Thomas, *My Lord, and my God!*

CHAPTER SIX

STUDY AND DISCUSSION GUIDE

1. The Greek word *apistia* is sometimes translated *doubt.* Explain its composition and what it means.

2. Explain why the disciples could not cast the *unclean spirit* [demon] out of the boy. Matthew 17: 17; Matthew 10: 1

3. Explain the meanings and applications of the Greek word *diakrino* as translated *doubt.* See Mark 11: 23

4. Discuss lessons surrounding Jesus' promise regarding casting a mountain into the sea. Do you believe that promise? Discuss.

5. Explain the Greek work *distazo,* translated *doubt.* What does it mean, and how is it manifested? Matthew 14: 25-31.

6. Consider the way doubt affects you. Discuss:
   - *Apistia*
   - *Diakrino*
   - *distazo*

CHAPTER SEVEN

SPIRITUAL ENEMY #2: DOUBT, PART 2

DEFEATING THE PROBLEMS OF LIFE

We began a consideration of doubt, in our last chapter, by dealing with what doubt is. Moving along, we will consider what God thinks about doubt; some causes of doubt; the results of doubt, and its solution.

GOD'S VIEW OF DOUBT

God calls doubt, unbelief *(apistia, distrust) evil.* I call your attention to these words found in the book of Hebrews: *Beware, brethren, lest there be in any of you an evil heart of unbelief (apistia), which leads to departing from the living God.* (Hebrews 3: 12).

Williams, in his outstanding translation of the New Testament, translates this reference as a *wicked, unbelieving heart.* Thus God considers doubt, unbelief, and distrust as abominable, wicked, and evil. Better than an incomplete definition, we will profit by looking at some examples, which will reveal varying aspects of God's view of *doubt.*

Recall how Jesus, as He was returning to Jerusalem at one point, encountered a fig tree without fruit on it. After cursing it, resulting in its withering away, He said to His disciples, *If you have faith and do not doubt, you will not only do what I have done . .* (Mt. 21:18- 22)

Here is a clear illustration that *doubt* is the very opposite to faith, thus displeasing to God: *if you have faith and do not doubt . .*

Recall again the account of how God sent three men to Joppa, apparently Italian Gentiles, to bring Peter to a small band of Italian Gentiles. Peter, being a Jew and somewhat racist oriented, would find such an imvitation as the most unlikely thing to appeal to him. They were heathen, barbarian outsiders, as far as Peter was concerned. In the face of potential resistance on Peter's part, God instructed him, *Arise, therefore, go down and go with them, **doubting nothing,** for I have sent them.* (Acts 10: 20)

No questions, Peter, just go! But Father, are you sure? No doubt, get on shanks mare and go – no more of your doubts! Whatever, it is clear that God abhors doubt. He demands simple obedience and trust.

The heart builds on the foundation of doubt; deceiving and causing the individual to disobey the Master's simple statement, *If you love me keep my commandments.* (John 14: 15)

He is saying, Believe, repent, and when you do, obey: be baptized, confess, come, follow, bear, give, pray, lay down your life; and the greatest command of all, love God and your neighbor.

Doubt says, I can't love my neighbor because he is unlovely, with a possible church division beginning, all because the individual doubts the ability to love! God despises this attitude. He says, *Behold, to obey is better than sacrifice . . . .* (I Samuel 15: 22)

God hates doubt, and its by-product, disobedience. John wrote, *He who does not believe (apistuo) God has made him a liar, because he has not believed . . . .* (I John 5: 10). When one questions the Lord's stated will in doubt or unbelief, he is guilty of calling the Lord a liar. Hard words, but true.

THE CAUSE OF DOUBT

The first cause: *an **over dependence on the natural and material*** realm produces doubt. Such a problem is exemplified by the statement, *Seeing is believing.* Here was Thomas' problem. When told that Jesus had risen from the dead, his reply: *Unless I see in His hands the print of the nails, and put my finger into [feel] the print of the nails, and put my hand into [feel] His side, I will not* *believe.* (John 20: 25). Thomas was fixated on feeling and see-ing, touch and sight, leading him to doubt or disbelief!

If he could not experience the truth with his five senses, with sight and touch, he refused to believe. Here was the problem of Russia's first astronaut, who looked into space from his Sputnik, and because he didn't see God, concluded that He didn't exist.

What if you ruled out everything you have not seen? Have you seen an atom? Have you seen the planets Saturn, Pluto, Uranus? Have you seen the gold in Fort Knox? Have you seen any oxygen lately?

Doubt comes because the individual is so settled on the natural that he cannot comprehend the spiritual, thus cannot perceive that he is actually a spirit, the flesh disguising the spirit.

Man has depended on the physical and material so much to supply his needs that he cannot understand how God can supply spiritually. He is squeezed into the world's mold (Romans 12: 1), and just by force of habit turns to the material rather than to God.

Remember, I wrote about the time my pocket had a hole in it? I was so accustomed to trusting my pocket that I carelessly and thoughtlessly dropped my change into that pocket, rather than putting it in a pocket I trusted! So it is that man is so settled in the world of the material, that he trusts it, resulting in doubt of God and His promises.

Secondly, *ignorance* is also a cause of doubt. Men keep them-selves in the dark, and as a result are incapable of understanding the light. The Word of God tells us, *And the light shines in the dark-ness, and the darkness did not comprehend it.* (John 1: 5). Why? The answer comes in John 3: 19, [because] *men loved darkness rather than light because their deeds (lifestyle) were evil.* Spiritual darkness results from a lack of knowledge of God's word, a lack of fellowship with the Father in prayer, and a lack of dependence on God.

Such a self-imposed darkness results in a lack of understand-ing of God's purpose, plan and dealings relating to man's daily life. Such was true of Job's wife, who, in the midst of suffering said,

Curse God and die. A lack of understanding led to this anger toward God.

This ignorance of God's ways hides and disguises how *all things work together.* So, when difficulties or suffering comes, doubts result. We should know, as an unknown poet wrote:

> *Not until each loom is silent*
> *And shuttles cease to fly,*
> *Will God unroll the pattern*
> *And explain the reason why?*
> *The dark threads are as needful,*
> *In the weaver's skillful hand*
> *As the threads of gold and silver*
> *In the pattern he had planned.*
> *(Author unknown)*

For a lack of understanding, many Christians are taken captive, locked behind the bars of *doubting castle,* as illustrated in Bunyan's *Pilgrims Progress.* Christian, in *Pilgrims' Progress*, was taken captive by Giant Despair, in doubting castle. After carelessly sleeping in Giant Despair's domain, Christian and his companion, Hopeful, were cast into the dungeon of doubting castle, and there, in such despair, Christian said, *The life that I now live is miserable. For my part, I know not whether it is best to live thus, or to die out of hand; my soul chooseth strangling rather than life, and the grave is more easy for me than the dungeon.*

Ignorance of God's word, and promises, lead to the dungeon of Doubting Castle, and cast the Christian down to defeat in despair.

Thirdly, the *presence of **unforgiven sin*** causes doubt. *But the natural man does not receive the things of the Spirit of God, for they are foolishness to him; nor can he know them, because they are spiritually discerned.* (I Cor. 2: 14); and the Christian, living in sin, in carnality, is in a similar predicament. The Apostle Paul wrote, *and I brethren, could not speak to you as spiritual people, but as carnal [flesh controlled], as to babes in Christ [immature]* . . (I Cor. 3: 1)

Fourth, **disobedience** leads to doubt. Christians doubt as an alibi in explaining away obvious requirements of God's. They are continually plagued by the Serpent's question of Eve, *Has God indeed said, 'You shall not eat of every tree of the garden?'* Did God really say . . .? He really didn't mean that for me, did He?

Did God really say that every Christian should be a witness? Has he said that *every* Christian has a gift of the Spirit to exercise? One doesn't really need to be immersed in baptism, does one? All of these questions, and then comes the reply in doubt. God didn't say that to me. Or the person might reply, in an effort to be scholarly, the Greek language means something different; He doesn't require that of every Christian. Or how about this one: *It really isn't important or essential?*

Here are just a few reasons why Christians doubt. You can probably add to the list.

THE RESULTS OF DOUBT

One, doubt results in **defeat**. Because of doubt, Peter began to sink and couldn't walk on the water, defeated by the stormy wind, defeated by doubt that he could really walk on the water. The Disciples were defeated in their effort to cast out the unclean spirit because of doubt, or unbelief. Consequently, Christians are defeated when they see the storms of life, when they are faced by great temptations, when they are confronted by mountainous problems. They sink in seas of problems; they are overwhelmed by unclean spirits; they are buried under the mountains of afflictions, suffering, sorrow, and difficulties.

I had just completed editing the previous chapter, and picked up a novel to read a short time before sleep. I started with page one, and when I came to the second paragraph, I encountered words that sent an alerting shock through my mind, as though I had put my finger into a 220 watt electrical outlet. Those words graphically described one's condition when suddenly overcome with doubt. In the face of a sudden crisis of disbelief, the book's main character said, *a cold numbness suddenly enveloped me. It was like I was on the other side of the aquarium window. I moved as though I was under water – back and forth, back and forth. . . .*

I saw in these words a graphic response to sudden doubt. The individual, filled with indecision, unable to find a firm foundation, immobilized by a divided mind, is suddenly set adrift on a sea of uncertainty and defeat. Here is the immobilizing effect when you or I suddenly are beset with doubts about the trustworthiness of God!

Doubt defeats. God commanded His people to go in and possess the land which He had promised to them, but because they doubted, they were defeated, seeing themselves *like grasshoppers* in comparison to the *giants* in the land.

Second, doubt leads to **disobedience,** as we have already discovered in the failure of the Israelites to obey God, by not entering to possess the land.

Pharaoh said, *Who is the Lord that I should obey His voice to let Israel go? I know not the Lord; neither will I let Israel go.* Pharaoh's unbelief led to disobedience, and the disobedience led to the ten most terrible plagues, culminating in the death of all of the Egyptian first born.

Third, we find *a whole bundle* of consequences of doubt: **fruitlessness, ruin, and suffering** – all adding up to sin. You can make a list of your own: Failure to plant because rain is doubted; failure to go out to battle because victory is doubted. You get the picture.

Finally, the sinner's doubt (unbelief) leads to **death**. *The wages of sin is death.* (Romans 6: 23) Death, eternal punishment and separation from God is the payoff for unbelief. *He who does not believe the Son shall not see life, but the wrath of God abides on him.* (John 3: 36)

I am reminded of the old story about a passenger boat threatening to sink in a stormy sea, because the engine suddenly stopped. An elderly lady rushed up to the captain and asked anxiously, *Is there any danger? Madam,* replied the captain, *we must trust God. Oh sir,* wailed the elderly inquirer, *has it come to that?*

Yes, it *has* come to that. People are willing to trust everything – except God. Try trusting God if you want to defeat this private enemy!

CHAPTER SEVEN

STUDY AND DISCUSSION GUIDE

1. What is God's view of doubt? Hebrews 12: 3; Acts 10: 20; I John 5: 10.

2. What was the cause of Thomas' doubt? John 20: 25.

3. What happens when your focus is too much on the material and physical?

4. Read John 1: 5 and 3: 19. What is the cause of doubt in these verses? Discuss and elaborate.

5. What caused Pilgrim's problem, in the excerpt from *Pilgrims Progress* quoted in this chapter? Tell the story and discuss the moral to the story.

6. What was the serpent's approach in getting Eve to doubt? Discuss how he uses that approach in your life.

7. Name some results of doubt and discuss.

CHAPTER EIGHT

PRIVATE ENEMY #2: DOUBT, PART 3

DEFEATING THE PROBLEMS OF LIFE

Doubt, a sophisticated term for *unbelief*, or Christian atheism, is well defined on the *most hated list* as a private enemy in the life of a Christian; and is the evil *well* from which many other problems spring up and defeat. Perhaps doubt should almost be rated as *Private Enemy #1,* since *doubt* really cancels, or serves as the cause of other problems. Consequently, my classifications are subject to some *tweaking.*

We have defined *doubt*, in its New Testament usage, as *unbelief, indecision, hesitation*, and so much more, in our relationship with God. God calls doubt evil and wicked, its being caused by: an over dependency on the material and physical (flesh!); ignorance of the will and blessings of the Father; unforgiven sin and disobedience – a self-imposed condition; resulting in defeat and disobedience for the Christian, and death for the unbeliever.

In the light of that condemning judgment, it behooves us to find:

THE SOLUTION TO DOUBT

Jesus' admonition to Thomas is our theme for this section, as we further find *how to defeat the problems of life*: *Be not faithless, but believing,* our admonition from the words of Jesus to Thomas.

There may be many more facets to this answer which we will consider, but if you will apply what is given here, you will be well on your way to *Defeating the Problems of Life*.

PROPER MOTIVATION

The first solution is simply **proper motivation**: you must be properly motivated, that is, have a real desire to rid yourself of the plague of doubt. Like an alcoholic faced with quitting that diabolical habit, if successful in quitting, he must first want to quit! So it is that the Christian seems to be driven to doubt, with an inner compulsion, like the alcoholic is driven to his next drink; his compulsions couched, hidden in his arch enemy, addiction to the *flesh*.

Just as the alcoholic has no cure 'til he recognizes his compulsion, and sincerely desires to give up devil drink; so no Christian will ever give up doubting 'til he recognizes the problem, and is sincerely motivated to release it from his life.

You see, doubt is the addiction to alibis that justify disobedience to the will of God, addicted to the life of carnality (the flesh). Just like the immature members of the church at Corinth were plagued with problems, as Paul wrote, *and I brethren, could not speak to you as spiritual people but as to carnal, as to babes in Christ . . . for you are still carnal . . . . where there are envy, strife, and divisions . . . .* (I Cor. 3: 1, 3)

The Corinthian believers were in that condition because they chose to be, not yet having the desire to kick their habit to the flesh – carnality.

So, to be properly motivated, you must be driven by:

LOVE!

Be motivated by your **love for God**; then you will desire to please Him. *We love Him, because He first loved us.* (I John 4: 19) – a love that sent our Savior to the cross.

Be motivated, knowing that the Savior, Himself, is watching and cheering you on.

At one point in my life, my wife had been after me for months, even years, to exercise, to stay in good physical condition. The only exercise I was getting was walking from the car to the office door, plus my table muscles at the dinner table!

However, I finally got started exercising, motivated by the love of my beloved wife, Jeanie. She cheered me on, and others cheered, too. I was jogging around the athletic field behind the church, when the high school students of Baymonte Christian School were moving from one building to another. Watching me jog, they began to clap; *Ray Pastor Culwell,* they cheered. One or two even accused me of getting ready for the Olympics. You know what happened; I turned on the speed, adding an extra lap around the field!

It really felt good, pleasing my wife; and those young people were an added bonus. However, the real key was Jeanie's love for me, coupled with my love for her. Yet, a higher motive should have been my love for my Savior, as Paul wrote to the Corinthians, *For the love of Christ compels us. . . . (2 Corinthians 5: 14),* writing further,

> *But I discipline my body and bring it into*
> *subjection lest when I have preached to*
> *others, I myself should become disqualified.*
> *(I Cor. 9: 27)*

Have you ever seen a young man or young woman whose lives seem to be so disappointing, feeling that life is hardly worth living? They find life horribly dull, common place, but when they fall in love, what a change in their attitude takes place! So it is when one falls in love with Jesus. What a change takes place; doubt and indecision disappear.

Be properly motivated by the love and encouragement of your Father in heaven.

OBEY

The second solution: overcome doubt with **simple obedience**, obeying God the very moment you discern His will.

As the Lord was teaching, a woman recognizing His excellence said, *Blessed is the womb that bore you, and the breasts which nursed you!* But Jesus said, *more blessed are those who hear the word of God and keep it.* (Luke 11: 27, 28)

Hearing the word of God and keeping [obeying] it – that's a key to dispelling doubt.

When Peter was summoned by the Gentile Cornelius to meet with his group of gentiles, there may have been reason for Peter to *wonder* about the summons, but the Holy Spirit told him, *Arise therefore, go down . . . doubting nothing;* just *obey* God and go! (Acts 10: 17, 20); and Peter obeyed and went, in spite of the fact that his very nature militated against it!

God would say to Abraham, *In your seed all the nations of the earth shall be blessed, **because you have obeyed** my voice.* (Genesis 22: 18) The nations would not be blessed because he had performed some mighty deed, because he was a man of great prowess, intellect, or excellence, but just *because he obeyed [God's] voice.*

The Bible says, *To obey is better than sacrifice, and to hearken than the fat of rams.* (I Sam. 15: 22)

Anne Sullivan had undertaken the seemingly impossible task of teaching the blind and deaf Helen Keller to talk, when Helen was at the age of six. She said to a friend, *I saw clearly that it was useless to try to teach [Helen] language or anything else until she learned to obey me. I have thought about it a great deal, and the more I think the more certain I am that obedience is the gateway through which knowledge, yes, and love too, can enter the mind of a child.*

Get into practice of giving simple obedience, whenever recognizing God's will, and doubt will disappear like a sneeze on a windy day. Remember, when the supply of wine was running out at the marriage at Cana, to supply more wine, the servants were told by Jesus to fill the water pots, which held water for washing feet. What an odd bit of instruction; what good would that do? Mary said to the servants, don't worry about those odd instructions, just do it If you desire to dispel doubt, as Mary said to those servants, *Whatever He asks you to do, do it*!

THE COMPANY YOU KEEP

The third solution in dispelling doubt, which I propose: subdue doubts by ***walking in the presence of the Savior***, delving daily into His Word, communicating consistently with Him in prayer.

When Thomas was *absent* at that first appearance of the risen Savior, he was overtaken with *doubt*, in spite of the words of validation given by the other ten Disciples. When told by them that Jesus had risen from the dead, and had been seen by them, Thomas said, *Unless I see in His hands the print of the nails, and put my finger into the print of the nails, and put my hand into His side, I will not believe.* (John 20: 25) He said, I've gotta see, feel, and touch before I believe. Yet, had Thomas been *present*, neither would have been required, for he would have seen the risen Savior! The intimate, personal presence of the Savior dispelled Thomas' doubt, and led him to respond, *My Lord and my God.* (John 20: 28)

Doubts will come, but you need not entertain them. As Martin Luther once said, *You can't keep the birds from flying over your head, but you can keep them from nesting in your hair.* All that is needed is an exercise of the will. *I will not doubt.*

Here was Job's approach in the midst of his suffering, *Though He slay me, yet will I trust Him.* (Job 13: 15)

Constant fellowship in the presence of the Lord Jesus Christ will deal decisively with doubts. Here is the value of one's presence in the church assembly, as we are admonished, *Forsake not the assembling of yourselves together . . . .* (Hebrews 10: 25)

A statue of a Greek slave girl stood in the marketplace of an Italian city, centuries ago. It represented the slave as tidy and well dressed. A ragged, uncombed little street girl, coming across the statue in play, stopped and gazed at it in admiration. Moved by sudden inspiration, as the story is told, she went home, washed her face and hair. Each time she looked at the statue she got a new idea, seeing beauty to admire and copy, until she was transformed.

By spending time in the Lord's presence, the believer is changed into His image.

But we all, with unveiled face, beholding as
in a mirror the glory of the Lord, are being
transformed into the same image from glory to
glory, just as by the Spirit of the Lord. (II Cor. 3: 18)

As the author of the hymn, *Take Time to Be Holy,* wrote: *By looking to Jesus, like Him thou shalt be.*

DEAL WITH SIN

The fourth solution to doubt we will consider: Resolve the problem of doubt by **dealing with sin**, not permitting unconfessed, unforgiven sin to stand between you and God.

The Prophet Daniel *purposed in his heart that he would not defile himself . . . .* (Dan. 1: 8); He determined to be free of the dominance of sin. Consequently, we read concerning Daniel, that he was a man of *excellent spirit, knowledge, understanding . . . and dissolving of doubts. . . .* (Daniel 5: 12, KJV)

Stay close to the Lord, pray, dig deeply into His Word for truth; deal with the sin problem; confess sin to God for forgiveness and cleansing (I John 1: 9), and doubts will last about as long as an ice cream come on a hot summer day!

On the other hand, keep your eyes on the world, and doubts will multiply like a brace of rabbits in Mr. Fudd's garden.

I have walked for exercise and health for decades. For two of those decades I walked down South Navarra Drive, past the industrial park on Green Hills Road, over the hills and valleys to Glen Canyon Road and back.

One day, while walking past the area where cars were parked, in front of industrial buildings, I began noticing coins often lying on the pavement where workers got in and out of their cars. I began walking with my head down, looking for change, pennies, nickels, dimes, and at times even quarters. Then, when I walked other places, my eyes were on the ground. One day I woke up to the fact that, while picking up pennies, I was missing the joys of drinking in the sight and glories of God's creation.

So it is, when we keep our eyes on the dregs of sin, the *pennies* of life, doubt flourishes as we miss the joy of walking with the Lord! Sin leads to doubt, robbing us of delighting in our Savior's presence, like walking with your head down, looking for pennies.

PRACTICING FAITH

The fifth and final solution to doubt considered in this treatise: Defeat doubt by practicing **walking by faith**.

Faith is the overriding recourse and foundation of every suggestion we have considered. There is no solution for any problem apart from faith. The just shall walk *by faith*! As Jesus said to blind Bartimaeus, *Your faith has made you whole.* (Mark 11: 46-52) Living faith, in the Lord, always makes one whole, no matter the problem.

The faith of the centurion brought healing to his servant, as Jesus said; *I say to you, I have not found such faith, not even in Israel,* at which time they *found the servant well.* (Luke 7: 8-10)

Remember the woman with an issue of blood, who touched the hem of Jesus' garment saying, *If only I may touch His clothes, I shall be made well,* and *immediately . . . she was healed of the affliction.* (Mark 5: 28, 29). So it is that the Lord heals doubt when we touch Him by faith. When the 12 year old daughter of the synagogue's ruler lay at the threshold of death, the Master said, *Be not afraid, only believe.* (Mark 5: 36). When faced with the dry-rot of doubt, threatening the foundation of life, these are the words we need.

THE SOURCE OF FAITH

What is the source of needed faith? The Bible says, *So faith comes by hearing, and hearing by the word of God.* (Romans 10: 17). God gives us His measure of faith as the Word is heard, received, and applied.

Long years ago a whole village of 60 families in Armenia embraced Islam under threat of torture and death. There was one exception, however, a woman aged 110 refused saying, *I am too old to deny my Lord.* The fierce Turks snatched her Bible from her hands, tore it to pieces, and burned the pages. She responded very calmly by saying, *You can do that, but you cannot tear its promises out of my heart.*

The source of faith: **Plant** the promises of God in your heart; and then the Holy Spirit will take that seed, producing faith.

Next, make it a **practice** to exercise faith in your life. As we say, *practice makes perfect.*

Then **rest** in that faith, visualizing the ultimate victory that is assured when you do.

Charles Allen, in his excellent book, *Life More Abundant*, wrote: *The architect gains strength for a long, tedious drawing because he pictures in his mind the completed cathedral. Columbus had strength to overcome opposition, to keep sailing west, in spite of conditions that would have caused almost any person to give up and quit because, in his mind, he pictured land ahead.*

Rest in faith, knowing there is land ahead, that the final victory is yours.

I've often given an exercise for rest to those having difficulty at times in sleeping, building the solution on the 23rd Psalm, *Count the promises of the Shepherd, rather than counting sheep, meditating on one word at a time;* I advise, *and sleep will come as you find rest in God.*

I gave this advice in a little church in Santa Cruz, California, I think, in 2002. A short time later, my sister-in-law Katy sent an e-mail to me, telling me that a lady visiting with her recently, hearing that advice nine years earlier, had taken that advice and had been sleeping well since!

The solution to doubt: First, proper motivation; then, simple obedience; next, walk with the Savior; again, deal with the sin problem; and finally, saturate it all with faith – trust God. *Only fear the Lord, and serve Him in truth with all your heart; for consider what great things He has done for you.* (I Samuel 12: 24).

Christian and Hopeful had been taken captive, and cast into Doubting Castle, wrote Bunyan in *The Pilgrim's Progress.* After much suffering and extended imprisonment, Christian said, in sudden realization, *What a fool am I, thus to lie in this stinking dungeon, when I may as well walk in liberty! I have a key in my bosom called PROMISE, that I will, I am persuaded, open any lock in Doubting Castle.*

With this, Christian plucked out the key called *Promise*, his all along, and opened the gates to freedom from Doubting Castle.

Now he and Hopeful could journey on in freedom and victory, on the King's Highway.

What a fool one is to stay in bondage to doubt, when the key of faith is in their possession for immediate deliverance.

Be not faithless, but believing!

CHAPTER EIGHT

STUDY AND DISCUSSION GUIDE

1. Can you recall Jesus' admonition to Thomas? Repeat it and discuss Thomas' problem.

2. What is the first step in the solution to doubt? I Cor. 2: 1, 3).

3. Name the second step in the solution to doubt and discuss. I John 4: 19; 2 Cor. 5: 14.

4. What is the third suggested step in solving the problem of doubt? Acts 10: 17, 20; Luke 11: 27, 28; I Samuel 15: 22.

5. How will *the company you keep* resolve the problem of doubt? John 20: 25, 28; Hebrews 10: 25; 2 Cor. 3: 18.

6. Another solution to the problem of doubt was illustrated by the author's experience while walking. Recount the example and the lesson involved.

7. What was the last solution given to the problem of doubt? Luke 7: 8-10; Mark 5: 36.

8. Consider the source of faith again and discuss. Romans 10: 17.

CHAPTER NINE

SPIRITUAL ENEMY #3: GUILT

Why do people feel so inferior, Ken Poure, Director of Hume Lake Christian Conference Center, asked while preaching in our church, to which he answered, *because they are.*

My question: why do people feel so guilty? I arrive at a similar answer as that given by Ken: they feel guilty because they are! The Bible says,

> *Now we know that whatever the law says*
> *it says to those who are under the law, that*
> *every mouth may be stopped, and all the*
> *world may be guilty before God. (Romans 3: 19)*

The word above translated *guilty* is *hupodikos,* which is otherwise translated *under the judgment* of God in the New King James translation. Thus, on the basis of *guilt*, all men are under the judgment of God. This is true because, as we read in verse 23 following: *All have sinned and fall short of the glory of God.*

Thinking about the problem of guilt, we turn to find the serious nature of its consequences, in David's cry:

> *For my iniquities have gone over my head;*
> *like a heavy burden they are too heavy for me.*
> *My wounds are foul and festering because of my*
> *foolishness. (Psalm 38: 4-5)*

If that is not enough, as David cries out about the burden of guilt in his life, his cries continue for sixteen more verses in that Psalm! Such is the nature of guilt!

Here is the cry of a deeply troubled, guilty soul. No doubt David's past sin with Bathsheba, in adultery, and his murder of her husband Uriah, including the failures in his own family, all weighed heavily upon him, all pointing to the two-fold problem man faces: one, real guilt, or two, guilt from the past that should no longer be an issue, because it has all been settled by the cross.

Do David's words possibly express how you feel? Note these words of David, surrounded by those just quoted:

> *There is no soundness in my flesh . . . or any*
> *health in my bones because of my sin. (Psalm 38: 3)*
> *I am troubled, I am bowed greatly. I go mourning*
> *all day long. (Psalm 38: 6)*

Oh, there is no weight like that of guilt. Guilt is like a dark cloud dropping great drops of rain on a gloomy day; like a great mountain slide of thundering rocks on tender blades of grass in a quiet mountain valley; like the crushing weight of death in the midst of anguish and sorrow.

Who is it who has not cried with King David, under the crushing burden of guilt: *I am troubled; I am bowed down greatly; I go mourning all day long.* (Psalm 38: 6)

Such a feeling may be well for the sinner, but is wholly unfitting for the saint. God does not desire that His children be burdened down and defeated by guilt. It is not His plan that they go about their valleys of dry bones, crying, *woe is me, for I am undone. . .* (Isaiah 6: 5). I am just a poor, weak sinner . . . wallowing in my slough of despondency.

No, His plan for us is that we have *faith* and *a good conscience* . . . . (I Timothy 1: 19)

If man is to have a *good conscience*, he must *defeat the problem of guilt*. The aim of all that is written, from this point concerning guilt, is written to lay bare the problem, emphasize how to be liberated from guilt, not by just dismissing the problem and its cause, but by finding deliverance from God.

However, remember that man *is* guilty! The solution is not to ignore this truth, hoping it will go away, but in finding the solution and deliverance from God.

THE PROBLEM

The problem is that, unresolved guilt is destructive, despairing, damning, defeating; AND Christians are highly susceptible to the problem.

Charles Haddon Spurgeon said concerning the destructive force of guilt, in reference to David's words,

> *For mine iniquities are gone over my head:*
> *like waves of the deep sea, like black mire*
> *in which a man utterly sinks. Above my hopes,*
> *my strength, and my life itself, my sin rising in*
> *its terror.*

TWO KINDS OF GUILT

We must recognize that there are two kinds of experiences of guilt.

Valid Guilt

One, guilt is a valid experience in the life of the unredeemed, in the life of that one who has not accepted the Redeemer's remedy for sin, having not realized that, *all have sinned and fall short of the glory of God.* (Romans 3: 23)

This person *should feel as guilty* as an old hound-dog caught sucking eggs, like our dog, old Alkali Pete, there on the farm in West Texas. When the eggshells were found and dad yelled *Alk,* he ran under the house in guilt. Nothing like an *egg-sucking* dog!

Two, guilt is valid in the life of a Christian who harbors unfor-given sin in his life, refusing to permit the Savior from taking over and cleansing it.

My closet is bulging at the seams, filled with clothes and shoes I will never wear. It needs to be cleaned, but I give it a look, close the doors (if there is room enough for them to close), and put off cleansing for another time.

Now, just like that closet, so Christians harbor unforgiven, hidden sins in their lives; shuffles them about, pushes them back out of sight, like the old clothes and shoes in the closet, sin eating away at his life, disaster and defeat resulting.

Guilt is valid in the face of unforgiven, unconfessed sin; and in this condition, the individual ought to feel as guilty as Old Alkali Pete caught sucking eggs! Guilt, under the conviction of the Holy Spirit, should relentlessly track such a person down like a bloodhound in pursuit of an escaped convict.

Invalid Guilt

Next, consider the invalid experience of guilt, this being the major problem with which we are concerned.

God's will is that the believer is to stand before Him *blameless* – guilt free! Paul wrote to the folks at Thessalonica,

> *Now may the God of peace Himself sanctify*
> *you completely. And may your whole spirit,*
> *soul, and body be preserved* **blameless** *at the*
> *coming of our Lord Jesus Christ. (I Thess.5: 23).*

Such is the inherited and rightful position of the redeemed, as we read; *There is therefore now no condemnation to those who are in Christ Jesus, who do not walk according to the flesh, but according to the Spirit.* (Romans 8: 1)

> *The individual in Christ is to be of a good con-*
> *science. (I Tim. 1: 5, 19).*

Examples of Invalid Guilt

One, guilt is invalid when a result from an ***incorrect value system*** that says that *man must* be guilty. One of the greatest problems, experienced by a new convert, is this one. He comes to Christ, but cannot believe that his sins are instantly cleansed. He is told, *If* *any man be in Christ, he is a new creature: old things have passed away; behold all things have become new.* (2 Cor. 5: 17).

He cannot believe it. Surely one must feel guilty and suffer for his own sins.

Another Christian is told, *If [you] confess [your] sins, God is faithful and just to forgive [your] sins, and to cleans [you] from all unrighteousness.* (I John 1: 9).

How many people are there who don't believe and practice that? A prevailing value system disputes this simple remedy; and says, *man must feel guilty*, ie, Man must be miserable over his sins. Man must agonize and wrestle with God before they can be relieved of guilt.

What if I were to say to my children: "You must wrestle and agonize with me every day before I will feed and clothe you? If you can beat me in arm-wrestling, you can have breakfast? Lunch is yours in exchange for a bucket of tears, and dinner for an hour of agony; but you've really got to weep and wail."

Silly? Yes, but some Christians have such an attitude when it comes to securing God's forgiveness, so as to be free of guilt. Got to do *penance*, sack cloth and ashes, and give up smoking for Lent.

Such an attitude is like making sheep wrestle with the shepherd before he will take care of them! Jesus gave the answer to this view as He said,

> *If you then, being evil, know how to give*
> *good gifts to your children, how much more will*
> *your Father who is in heaven give good things*
> *to those who ask Him. (Matthew 7: 11).*

A prerequisite to the Christian life and ultimate forgiveness *is not* a guilty feeling. Oh no, some would rather say, I'm such a weak miserable sinner, as the Psalmist said,

> *I am troubled; I am bowed down greatly;*
> *I go mourning all the day long. (Psalm 38: 6).*

This is okay before you confess your sin, but not after you do!

Two, another attitude that is invalid says: There must be **things about which I don't know,** for which I must feel guilty. This person is upset because he doesn't have something for which he is over-whelmed in guilt.

This attitude comes with the desire for *self-justification* – paying for one's own sins. What does the Bible say about such an attitude?

> *Beloved, if our heart does not condemn us,*
> *we have confidence toward God. (I John 3: 21).*

Be open to the leading of God's Spirit, sensitive to God's word, and then *don't worry* about the unknown. We are responsible for the amount of light we have.

A mother visited our home many years ago, and before we looked, her child ate some of the cat's food off of the floor. Could we say the little child had sinned? What he had done might be unacceptable, but could we label it sin? No, for he knew no better. That child did not know that it was forbidden to eat the cat's food off of the floor. The child would learn, as he grew, and would learn even from this experience. The Bible says,

> *Therefore, to him who knows to do good*
> *and does not do it, to him it is sin. (James 4: 17)*

Don't impose guilt on yourself for things you do not know are wrong. On the other hand, be reminded that *self-imposed igno-rance is another issue.* One *does* need to shine the light of God's word on his deeds.

Three, it is invalid for the believer to try to **bear the guilt of others.** Here is what we are doing when we say, *Oh, it's all my fault. If I had (or hadn't) done that, he would have never . . . .*

We see such an attitude expressed in society. We *are* our brother's keeper; but look at the prevailing attitude about group or societal guilt. An assassination takes place, for example, and they judge the entire society as being guilty. We are all guilty, we are told. The Lord said, as found in Jeremiah, *Every man who eats the sour grapes, his teeth shall be set on edge.* (Jeremiah 31: 30)

THE CAUSE

Like a skilled diagnostician, let us get to the root of the problems, in order that, in the final analysis, we can remove the cause rather than just treat the symptoms.

One of our church members, after a long period of suffering, complained of his doctor's treatment. *All he does is give me pills to kill the pain, and that's not what I want. I want him to find the cause and remove that.*

Here is the reason we are dealing with the cause of guilt, as a problem, rather than just treating the symptoms, while the malignancy, undiscovered, goes about destroying the vitality of the victorious Christian life.

With that, we will examine some major causes of the guilt problem.

CAUSES OF INVALID GUILT

First, invalid guilt is a result of **the direct attack of Satan**. C. S. Lovett has accurately observed: *Clearly the center of our warfare [with] Satan is our mind. The only way to capture a man is to get him to think as you do. Ideas capture man, not weapons.*

Here is Satan's method of attack against man: He implements debilitating, defeating, destructive thoughts in the mind; and one of his major strategies is to get us to feel guilty, just another way of destroying confidence in God, *If our heart does not condemn us, we have confidence toward God.* (John 3: 24). So we are told, *Be sober, be vigilant; because your adversary the devil walks about like a roaring lion, seeking whom he may devour.* (I Peter 5: 8)

The wily serpent is dedicated to our destruction, and if guilt will do the job, then one may be sure of his attack. Here is the way that Satan accuses us in our minds: Remember when you took that money; told that lie; when you cheated in that trade; had that impure thought. What makes you think that God will bless such a sinner as you, with sin like that in your life? Just a sample of how Satan accuses us to ourselves.

We are sure of this kind of attack because the name *devil* comes from the Greek *diabolos,* meaning *accuser or slanderer.*

J. Dwight Pentecost of Dallas Seminary hit the nail on the head, as he wrote: *One of the adversary's tactics – since he cannot take away our salvation – is to take away the joy of our salvation. Since our sonship is settled, he seeks to keep us from enjoying it. One of his subtle methods of doing this is to remind us of some past sin. It may be something we did years ago which he delights to use to torment us. It may be something of which we were guilty before we ever came to know Jesus Christ as our Savior.*

Years ago a fine Christian man came to me from another city, sent by his pastor. He was so burdened and distraught, one would fear for his mental and emotional stability. However, a rather brief encounter was enough to give assurance that he had personally received Christ, and that the *accuser* had been so successful in his accusations that he seriously doubted his relationship with God.

How often has Satan brought unattractive events from your past life to mind, in an effort to convince you that you are a failure? At one point or another, he has focused my attention on almost everything about which I have been ashamed in my past.

An interesting factor, here, is that Satan used the words of an evangelist to trigger the accusation that led to the problem with the man referenced above, leading us to realize the *deceiver* will take words of truth, twist, misapply, so as to condemn and make us feel guilty. No wonder Satan is called *deceiver,* the word coming from the Greek, *Planeo,* which means to *lead astray* or *seduce.* (Revelation 12: 9)

He often uses human instruments to do his dirty work. Jesus said in His Olivet discourse, *Many false prophets shall rise, and shall deceive many.* (Matthew 24: 11). Here is a case of using false messengers and messages, not just twisting the truth.

Satan counterfeits the method of the Holy Spirit, accusing and producing false conviction, thus invalid guilt. He lies, and actually accuses us before God, as the Bible says, *For the accuser of our brethren is cast down, who accused them before God day and night.* (Rev. 12: 10)

Second, invalid guilt comes as a result of **Legalism,** one trying to live under the law rather than under grace. The law is designed to teach us about, and convict us of sin, so as to bring us to Christ. *Therefore the law was our tutor to bring us to Christ, that we might be justified by faith.* (Galatians 3: 24)

The word translated *tutor,* in the New King James translation, comes from the Greek word *paidagogos,* here carrying the connotation of *training and discipline*, thus resulting in guilt or conviction. The law, as designed to provide guilt, is to drive us to the grace of God; but once grace is found, we often pervert God's grace by returning to guilt under the law. Here is what was happening with the Galatian Christians, as the Apostle Paul wrote to them; *I marvel that you are turning away so soon from Him who called you in the grace of Christ, to a different gospel.* (Galatians 1: 6)

Correcting the Galatian error, the apostle would write, *For as many as are of the works of the law are under the curse. . . ; But that no one is justified by the law in the sight of God is evident, for* **the just shall live by faith.** (Galatians 3: 10, 11)

Look at this contrast between law and grace:

The law says, *Cursed is everyone who does not continue in all things which are written in the book of the law, to do them.* (Deuteronomy 27: 26)

On the other hand grace says: *But to him who does not work but believes on Him who justifies the ungodly, his faith is accounted for righteousness.* (Romans 4: 5)

Living legalistically, rather than by grace, results in a guilt-ridden life.

Three, invalid guilt comes from an ***attitude of inferiority***.

I may ask, why am I not like John Wesley, George Whitfield, or D. L. Moody? I see a church ministering to thousands and I might ask, why am I just reaching hundreds? I see crowds responding to an evangelistic invitation by Billy Graham, and I could ask, why can't I do that? Why can't I preach like that, teach like that, sing like that? The view of inferiority leads to a sense of guilt. There must be something wrong or lacking with me, is our conclusion.

The point is that God made me who I am, and placed me where He wants me. He didn't make me like George Whitfield or D. L. Moody. He made me, me! And then guilt comes, if I am not satisfied with who God made me, resulting from a sense of inferiority!

Think with me about how invalid that thought is. Imagine the 12 year old kid facing the 9 ft. tall giant, Goliath. What if David had said, *I'm too little; I'm not as big as he. He has a spear with a shaft as big as a weaver's beam, and I have only a puny sling with five little rocks.* All too often, here is the way we face life, a life of inferiority that leads to guilt, because we leave all the giants for someone else to kill!

However, not David, for he said, I've got my equalizer, *I come to you in the name of the Lord of hosts,* and quicker than Wyatt Earp or Wild Bill Hickok could draw their six-guns, he rubbed out that big boy with his rock and sling! No inferiority here, and consequently, no guilt.

Four, guilt comes with the **inability to forgive yourself**. You have failed; you come to Christ; He forgives you, but you can't forgive yourself. That failure is covered with a scab that you keep picking off, baring the wound to your soul. You won't permit God to take it away, and guilt gnaws away at you.

Behold, I give you the authority to trample on serpents and scorpions; Jesus said, *and over all the power of the enemy, and nothing shall by any means hurt you.* (Luke 10: 10)

This was a statement given to the seventy, sent out to accomplish a special task under His protective care. He wasn't just facing a cult of snake handlers. Now, we might make *symbolic* application and say that his promise is that you have power over these snakes and scorpions, meaning those sinister, deadly things that slither through your life and strike down and poison your soul – past sins that God has forgiven.

I've known many people over the years who had trouble forgiving themselves, tormented by serpents from the past, guilt laden, unhappy. This failure robs man of happiness, destroys marriages, and embitters souls.

A rich farmer of Ferrara, Italy left a major portion of his $1,600,000 estate to the Pope and the Roman Catholic Church. According to a statement made by lawyers who handled the estate, the will of Marion Magrini declared that he wanted his wealth to go to the papacy to atone for his sins.

He should have asked for a money-back guarantee, for atonement for sin cannot be achieved by the good works or charitable acts of man, but comes solely by the redemptive work of Christ on the cross.

August Toplady recognized this truth in his hymn, *Rock of Ages:*

> *Could my tears forever flow,*
> *Could my zeal no languor know,*
> *Those for sin could not atone;*
> *Thou must save, and Thou alone;*
> *In my hand no price I bring,*
> *Simply to Thy cross I cling.*

Guilt is such a waste and a superfluous possession for the blood-bought child of God.

The Apostle Paul, not only stood consenting to the stoning of Stephen, but hauled many into prison and to their deaths, in his misdirected zeal. He would write to Timothy, *This is a faithful saying, and worthy of all acceptance, that Christ Jesus came into the world to save sinners; of whom I am chief.* (I Timothy 1: 5). The Savior who cleaned and saved this *chief of sinners* can resolve the sin and guilt problem in your life – by faith!

CHAPTER NINE

STUDY AND DISCUSSION GUIDE

1. What are the two kinds of guilt? Romans 3: 23; I Thessalonians 5: 23; 2 Corinthians 5: 17.

2. Name and describe an invalid value system that leads to an invalid guilt, and the answer to that guilt. Matthew 7: 11; I John 3: 21.

3. What invalid guilt is described by I Peter 5: 8 and I John 3: 21? Discuss.

4. What was the problem in the church at Galatia that led to invalid guilt? Galatians 1: 6; Galatians 3: 24; 3:10, 11.

5. A feeling of _____ leads to a feeling of invalid guilt. Fill in the blank and discuss.

6. Guilt comes from the inability to _____ yourself. Fill in the blank and discuss. Luke 10: 19.

7. What truth do the words of the hymn *Rock of Ages* express? I Timothy 1: 5. Can you sing the hymn? Why not sing it, or if in a group, all sing!

CHAPTER TEN
PRIVATE ENEMY #3: GUILT, PART 2

For though you wash yourself with lye, and use much soap, yet your iniquity is marked before me, says the Lord God.

These were words spoken through the Prophet Jeremiah. One has commented in this connection: *If soap could cleanse iniquity, this ought to be the purest nation on earth, for the singing commercials have sold detergents until America's drowning in an ocean of soap suds.*

But the truth of the matter is, we can't cleanse ourselves, though so many social and governmental programs have tried, as we have a society weighted down with sin, weighted down like a flea with an elephant strapped on its back.

Christ has solved the sin and guilt problem forever, or has provided the solution; yet hundreds of thousands are being driven to psychiatrist's couches, drugs, drink, and mental institutions, with Christians joining the parade. In a recent decade the suicide rate has skyrocketed. During that period of time, the suicide rate in Los Angeles went up over 1,000% in ages under 20, and up over 300% in ages 20-29. Six percent in a survey, between the ages of 12-17, had tried heroin at least one time.

Because of guilt, valid or invalid, multitudes are defeated, like an unarmed hundred year old man faced by a tribe of terrorists armed with AK47s. Because of that guilt-burden, they find no purpose in life, thus are unproductive and weak. As the late Peter Marshall said, *Men garbed for deep sea diving . . . spend their time pulling plugs out of bathtubs.*

We must find the solution to the sin problem, and resultant guilt, private enemy that it is. That being true, we continue from the last chapter looking at the causes of guilt, followed by the results or consequences of guilt.

CAUSES, CONTINUED

First, some causes of invalid guilt are: The direct influence of Satan, the deceiver, both with and without the help of man, legalism, an attitude of inferiority, and an inability to forgive one's self.

Extending our consideration of the last named cause, the inability to forgive one's self, this individual feels that their guilt is too great for God's forgiveness.

Years ago an experiment was performed in which a plank 12 inches wide was placed on the ground, with an invitation to people to walk on it. After the people walked on it, the same plank was placed on supports high in the air, asking the same people to walk on it. Only a few dared to do so!

Many Christians are like that in relation to their sins. They feel that God can and will forgive a *little* sin, but if it is elevated so that it might be called a *big sin*, or *high up* on the list of sins, they are suddenly filled with fear that God either cannot or will not forgive it.

A well-supported plank is a plank whether on the ground or in the air; and sin is sin no matter the *size*. This truth is made clear in the book of James, where we are told; to violate one commandment is to be guilty of violating them all!

One degrades the forgiveness and blood of Christ in saying that any sin is too great, or any sinner too big for forgiveness!

The reason people won't walk a plank up in the air, which they will walk on the ground, is because: on the ground they think of *walking*; in the air they think of *falling*. So, with a *little* sin they are able to think *forgiveness*, while consumed with guilt over the *big sin,* they think only of *guilt and punishment*.

Before moving on, keep in mind the almost universal desire of man to be *self-sufficient,* causing him to feel that he is responsible, at least in part, for gaining his own forgiveness. He feels that he must pay a price, a feeling that ends up annulling the concept of grace. This brings us back to the words of Henley, as he said, *I am the master of my fate; I am the captain of my soul;* or as Protagoras said, *Man is the measure of all things.* The believer will not fully subscribe to either position, but still cannot relinquish himself completely to the grace of God. He, all too often, insists on retaining some measure of responsibility for himself.

The false cause of guilt, no matter how phrased, ends up with *self* being the guilty culprit, just as sure as John Dillinger was guilty of robbing banks.

VALID CAUSES

Very first on the list of valid causes of guilt is the **convicting power** of the Holy Spirit. We hear King David saying, *There is no soundness in my flesh because of your anger, nor any health in my bones because of my sin.* (Psalm 38: 3)

David experiences no rest, no peace, because of sin. God does this to the individual through conviction, as David said, *because of your [God's] anger.* As Augustine said, *Man is restless until he finds rest in thee, O God.*

In contrast to invalid guilt that is unjustly *self-imposed*, the result of guilt from conviction is the work of the *Holy Spirit. And when He [the Comforter, Paraclete, Holy Spirit] is come, He will reprove [convict, convince] the world of sin . . .* (John 16: 8). This convicting ministry comes into every life because *all have sinned.* (Romans 3: 23).

The mother eagle teaches her little ones to fly by making their nest so uncomfortable that they are forced to leave it, committing themselves to the unknown world of air outside. God does the same for us. He stirs us up in the conviction of the Holy Spirit, applying *guilt* to push us out of our comfortable nests of sin, and softness of inactivity.

Recognize the guilt induced by the Holy Spirit; and take God's remedy in confession and repentance, the solution to this type of guilt.

One, the Holy Spirit uses the *word of God* in inducing this conviction of guilt, *word* both written and spoken. It was in response to

Peter's sermon at Pentecost that we find conviction in response to the Word of God, *When they heard this, they were pricked in their heart,* and said to Peter and to the rest of the apostles, *Men and brethren, what must we do?* (Acts 2: 37). Do you feel guilty and restless at times in response to your pastor's words? If so, don't pass it off. Find what God wants you to do.

Two, the Holy Spirit also applies the **laws of God** to man's conscience in bringing him to the conviction of guilt. For example, James tells us, *If you show partiality, you commit sin, and are convicted by the law of transgressors.* (James 2: 9)

Paul adds that *the law was our tutor to bring us to Christ.* (Galatians 3: 24). *You can never appreciate the grace and mercy of God until you know what the law is all about.* (Bill Gothard) We measure our life as we look into the mirror of the law and God's word. *For if anyone is a hearer of the word and not a doer, he is like a man observing his natural face in a mirror; for he observes himself, goes away, and immediately forgets what kind of man he was.* (James 1: 22-24)

The mirror is the law and the word of God. Measure your life by considering it in the light of God's revealed will, your life as revealed in contrast with the expectations of obedience to government, your life in contrast with your responsibility to family, friends, self, and even others.

> *Do all things without complaining and disputing*
> *that you may become blameless and harmless*
> *children of God without fault in the midst of a*
> *crooked and perverse generation, among whom*
> *you shine as lights in the world. (Philippians 2: 14, 15)*

You look into the mirror and see these requirements, and when you fail to measure up, God's Holy Spirit brings conviction and guilt.

Second, **personal failure** leads to an inner guilt, which should drive one to God. Remember how the self righteous Pharisees brought the adulterous woman to Jesus to be judged, so as to trap Him? After Jesus had stooped to write in the sand, He said to them,

He who is without sin among you, let him throw a stone at her first. (John 8: 7).

As Jesus stooped to write in the sand again, we are told, *Then those who heard it [who heard His words] being convicted by their conscience, went out one by one . . . .* (John 8: 9). They were convicted of guilt, within, for their sin and failure. Too bad they didn't cry out for forgiveness, rather than slinking away like cowards!

Permit guilt from failure to draw you to God for forgiveness. Failure to do so and your guilt will defeat you and drive you away from the Savior.

Three, guilt results from a **lack of faith.** When you are faithless, you should feel guilty! *Beloved, if our heart does not condemn us (if we don't experience guilt), we have confidence toward God (and a clear conscience).* (I John 3: 21)

The man named Little Faith, in *Pilgrims' Progress,* sat down and went to sleep at the end of *Dead Man's Lane;* whereupon he was set upon by three thugs by the names of *Faint Heart, Mistrust,* and *Guilt* – all brothers. *Faint Heart* and *Mistrust* took *Little Faith's* possessions, and then Bunyan writes concerning Little Faith's *Guilt:* **Guilt,** *with a great club that was in his hand, struck* **Little Faith** *on the head, and with that blow felled him flat to the ground, where he lay bleeding as one that would bleed to death.*

Little faith does produce guilt, which does fall on us, and drains us of life's blood, like a vicious, ravenous leach latched on to your carotid artery.

Four, closely related to a lack of faith is *immaturity*, which is also inexcusable and produces guilt. Paul, speaking of some being offended because others were eating meat offered to idols, said *their conscience being weak, is defiled.* (I Corinthians 8: 7)

Five, another cause of guilt comes from **efforts to justify or excuse failure.** There are those who fail, and rather than permit God to deal with their failure through faith, choose rather to punish themselves with guilt, in an act of justifying what they are doing – substituting suffering for their own sin.

We have considered a few causes of guilt, guilt that drives us to defeat like lemmings being self driven into the sea.

CONSEQUENCES

As we turn to consider the results, the **consequences of guilt**, we find that there are varying consequences.

SPIRITUAL

First, there *are* dire, **spiritual consequences**. As we read from the 38th Psalm, *For my iniquities have gone over my head; like a heavy burden they are too heavy for me. My wounds are foul and festering because of my foolishness. I am troubled, I am bowed down greatly; I go mourning all the day long.* (Psalm 38: 4-6)

There is first the *loss of one's witness* through guilt. I like the *American Standard Revised Version* phrasing here, *but sanctify Christ as Lord in your hearts, always being ready to make a defense to everyone who asks you to give an account for the hope that is in you, yet with gentleness and reverence; and keep a good conscience so that the thing in which you are slandered, those who revile your good behavior in Christ may be put to shame.* (I Peter 3: 15, 16)

Aside from a natural conclusion, that guilt will obviously rob one of an effective personal witness. The implication here, in this passage, is that one will not be able to give a good witness and defense of their faith apart from a *clear conscience*.

PHYSICAL

Next, we find that there are dire **physical consequences** which result from guilt. It is hard to realize just how much our physical health is affected by our spiritual and mental condition. David says, as a result of his spiritual distress: *For my loins are full of inflammation, and there is no soundness in my flesh. I am feeble and severely broken; I groan because of the turmoil of my heart.* (Psalm 38: 7, 8)

Consider this paraphrase of David's words found in Psalm 32, verses 3 and 4:

> *There was a time when I wouldn't admit*
> *what a sinner I was. But my dishonesty made*

me miserable and filled my days with frustration.
All day and all night your hand was heavy
on me. My strength evaporated like water
on a sunny day.

The King James translation says, *My moisture is turned into the drought of summer.*

Attending a Basic Youth Conflicts seminar, perhaps 30 or more years ago, I heard Bill Gothard make this application of the passage just cited from Psalm 32.

Gothard said that American Indians applied the principle mentioned in Psalm 32 of *moisture turning into the drought of summer* in detecting a guilty person among their tribe. Here is Bill's statement:

When a crime was committed, they would
lock up all suspects. They would then heat
a knife. Each suspect was told to stick out
his tongue. The flat side of the knife was
put against the tongue for an instant, then
taken away. If the individual was innocent,
it [the knife] would not burn him; but if guilty, the
knife would burn his tongue.
The principle was that a guilty person's mouth
becomes dry, and therefore, the heat against
the dry tongue would burn it. On the other hand,
the innocent person's mouth and tongue would be
moist and the hot knife would only burn the
moisture into steam. Here is what happens when one
tests a hot iron by first licking his finger. The
heat only singes the water, not the finger!

Guilt does produce an adverse physical effect, resulting from a chemical change. David makes it absolutely clear in both the 32nd and 38th Psalms that sore physical distress had resulted from his guilt.

PSYCHOLOGICAL

Third, there are **psychological consequences** that result from guilt – **depression.** There have been those who have been so depressed with guilt that mental derangement has resulted, including turning to drink, drugs, and even suicide. David's depression was expressed in these words:

> *I am troubled,*
> *I am bowed down greatly;*
> *I go mourning all the day long. (Psalm 38: 6)*

The mind and emotions of mortal man cannot survive such depression of long duration.

SOCIAL

Fourth, there are **social** consequences of guilt, leading to exclusion and isolation. David, even while serving as King, suffered such consequences. He cried,

> *My loved ones and my friends stand aloof*
> *from my plague; and my relatives stand afar*
> *off. (Psalm 38: 11)*

CONCLUSION

An unusual meat eating plant grows in the mountain swamps of Norway, the *Sundew* plant. The swollen tip of each leaf is covered with glandular hairs; on each leaf is a drop of sweet, sticky liquid. When an insect, attracted to the liquid, crawls over a leaf, the plant enfolds the insect, and the plant's sweet, sticky secretion soon digests the insect.

Guilt is like that. It results from sin which seems to be sweet and tasty, but then devours its foe spiritually, physically, psychologically, and socially.

CHAPTER TEN

STUDY AND DISCUSSION GUIDE

1. Why will people walk on a plank on the ground, when they won't walk on it high in the air? Make application in relation to *little sin* and *big sin.*

2. What role does the Holy Spirit play regarding sin and guilt? John 16: 8; Romans 3: 23.

3. What purpose is served by resultant guilt from the work of the Holy Spirit? Discuss the result from Peter's sermon at Pentecost. Acts 2: 37. Discuss the example of an eagle teaching the young to fly.

4. What purpose does the law and word of God fulfill? James 2: 9; James 1: 22-24.

5. What is indicated by a lack of guilt when one is faced with disobedience to the will of God? John 3: 21.

6. Name some spiritual consequences resulting from guilt. I Peter 3: 15, 16; I John 3: 21.

7. What are some physical consequences resulting from guilt? Psalm 38: 7, 8; Psalm 32: 3, 4; Psalm 38: 6.

8. Discuss the Indians' test of guilt as related to the statement in Psalm 32: 3-4.

9. Are there social consequence resulting from guilt? If so, what are they? Psalm 38: 11.

CHAPTER ELEVEN

PRIVATE ENEMY #3: GUILT, PART 3

C. S. Lewis wrote that man is staggering between *Vanity Fair and Armageddon, between a mad pursuit of pleasure and excess, and the impending judgment of God.*

Part of the burden under which he staggers is that of *guilt;* and the solutions he pursues to alleviate the problem of guilt end up increasing the burden. When the temporary palliatives of the world wear off, man feels like a drunk with a hangover the morning after; or like the alcoholic in withdrawals with delirium tremens. The temporary solution has served only to intensify the problem.

For example, so-called *experts*, defined as drips, want to legalize the use of marijuana, under the pretext that it is harmless. Contrary to their view, four British doctors made a study of ten young adults who had smoked marijuana from 3 to 11 years, discovering brain damage. They found cerebral atrophy, or irreversible shrinking of brain tissue in the ten young men.

Marijuana use, like that of alcohol, is designed to supposedly lighten one's emotions and elevate a sense of euphoria, thus an escape from reality. As seen from the example above, the resultant escape is worse than the guilt from which the user is trying to escape.

When man tries to solve his own guilt problems without God's help, he ends up worse than he began. When he tries to expand his mind in a worldly manner, he may well end up shrinking it!

Such is the truth expressed by the Savior: *When an unclean spirit goes out of man, he goes through dry places, seeking rest, and finds none.* Then the unclean spirit says, *I will return to my house from which I came.* And when he comes, he finds that the house is empty, swept, and put in order. Then the unclean spirit goes and takes with him seven other spirits more wicked than him-self, and they enter and dwell there; *and the last state of that man is worse than the first.* (Matthew 12: 43-45)

I started smoking cigarettes, rolling my own *Bull Durham* and *Duke's Mixture*, at the ripe old age of thirteen, soon graduating to ready rolls *Lucky Strikes* and then *Camels*. As the *Camels* ad said, *I'd walk a mile for a Camel!* I determined to quit at the age of 20, all cold turkey, on my own. To assuage the desire for cigarettes, I took up eating snacks and chewing gum. The results: I began putting on weight, forming a new habit in replacing the old. Thus, I started smoking again so as to quit eating, and lose weight!

After meeting Jean Larum, my wife-to-be, I was challenged by her Christian life-style, and renewed my relationship with Christ. At that time I quit my two-pack of *Camels* a day habit, with God's help, with ease, and no need for a replacement!

We need to discover the *real solution* to the problem of guilt, not self-efforts in which we substitute one problem for another - our purpose beginning in this chapter.

THE SOLUTION

We began this pursuit in the last chapter, but now will deal with it under three headings: man's Efforts; God's Solution; and the practical application of that solution.

MAN'S EFFORTS

We begin by considering the **blind alleys** down which men go in search of their own solution to the problem of guilt. However, keep in mind that, as we will find later, the only lasting solution comes from God.

David recognized this truth, as he said,

> *For in You, O Lord, I hope; You will hear,*
> *O Lord my God. Make haste to help me,*
> *O Lord, my salvation! (Psalm 138: 15, 22)*

Keep firmly in mind, as David said, when it comes to the solution of guilt, one can only hope in the Lord, and find help and salvation in Him.

Thinking about my Navy (Marine) jet pilot grandson, I was reminded of the jet pilot that was coming in for a landing on an aircraft carrier. As he touched down, his hook failed to catch on the arrester cable. Realizing what had happened, he slammed the throttle open again, but by this time the plane was traveling slowly. The bystanders watched in alarm as the aircraft disappeared from view, as it fell over the bow of the carrier. Eventually it reappeared, its jets blasting furrows on the sea as it staggered along only a few feet above the water. As the jet finally began to gain height, a cool, clear voice came over the radio, *Alright God, I'll take over now!*

Just as this jet pilot realized that his deliverance depended on turning his ship over to God, we must realize that God is the only hope we have in keeping the ship of life from crashing under a load of guilt.

Still, man tries to solve the problems by himself. Paul, writing to Titus, deals with this attitude.

> *They profess to know God, but in works*
> *they deny Him . . . . (Titus 1: 16)*

One, man tries to dull the pain of guilt with the pursuit of **pleasure**, including alcohol, drugs, and sex, among other pursuits of the flesh. Consider just the first part of Isaiah 53: 6, *All we like sheep have gone astray;* **we have turned everyone, to his own way** *. . . .*

Recall that we found, in one survey, that 6% of those from ages 12 through 17 had tried heroin at least once. Add a few more statistics, uncovered by Response Analysis Corp. of Princeton, New Jersey. They found, in a survey of 3,186 persons, among the youth, that 10% had tried hashish, 8% LSD, peyote and mescaline, 5% cocaine, and 8% speed.

In a survey of unmarried girls, ages 15 to 19, by Temple University's Institute for Survey Research, it was discovered that: by age

15, 13.8% of the unmarried girls had sexual experience; 21.2% by age 16; 26.6% by age 17; 37.1% at age 18; 46.1% by age 19.

Many colleges and universities across America have open dorms, even permitting boys and girls to share the same room.

On the other hand, addiction to alcohol and drugs is common and rampant.

Second, others, in an effort to salve their own guilty consciences, turn to **activity, work, and even religion**. Do a little social good; create a little ritual; go to church where the preacher will give a sweet, little, superficial homily to sooth the conscience.

Even in the strongest of Bible-centered preaching, the cry of protest from the pew is: don't try to put me under a guilt trip – must not say anything to step on a toe! Things are no different now from what they have always been. Man would rather the preacher give them a *pat* rather than a *push*; a *compliment* rather than a *command* from God; a *pronouncement* of peace rather than *preach* judgment. *Make me feel good at any price. Give me a good, easy solution. Don't make me feel guilty, pronouncing the necessity of repentance needed to remove guilt,* expresses the prevailing attitude.

King Zedikiah shut Jeremiah up in prison, saying *Why do you prophesy and say, 'Thus says the Lord . . . .'* (Jeremiah 32: 2, 3) John the Baptist lost his head for telling Herod, *It is not lawful to have your brother's wife.*

J. H. Jowett spoke of Christians *running with the hares and hunting with the hounds* all at the same time. People want to provide their own solution for guilt while resorting to ridiculous ritual, loony liturgy, and trivial tasks.

I like what the old southern Baptist preacher, Vance Havener said, *We are not here to learn how to live in the dark, but how to walk in the light.*

Three, others try to **rationalize away** the cause of guilt, with such mental gymnastics as these: It happened too long ago, insignificant, small, and not important. Then there is the rationalization on the basis that *everybody is doing it,* thus making it okay for me. Vance Havener has the right quote once again, as he observed,

When the Lord's sheep are smudged in gray, the black sheep will feel more comfortable.

The hymn-writer furnishes the answer to such an attitude:

What can wash away my sin?
Nothing but the blood of Jesus.

Yet, best of all, leave it to the Scriptures: *Almost all things are purified with blood, and without the shedding of blood there is no remission.* (Hebrews 9: 22)

Man cannot justify nor solve his own guilt problem apart from God. Job is heard to say, *If I wash myself with snow water, and cleanse my hands with soap, yet you [God] will plunge me into the pit, and my own clothes will abhor me.* (Job 8: 30-31)

One day, a telephone line supervisor was standing outside the Chaplain's office on a Marine base in California, shouting instructions to his co-worker who was installing wire on the roof. Suddenly, the Chaplain came to the door and asked, *Sergeant, are you waiting to see me? No sir,* the Sergeant replied, pointing up toward his co-worker, *I was just talking to him.* The Chaplain looked at the Sergeant and smiled, *More people should. Bless you, my son.*

Yes, more people should look to God, rather than trying to solve their own guilt, knowing that Christ furnishes the absolute solution.

GOD'S SOLUTION

First, we deal with this topic **doctrinally**, seeing as we do, God's perfect solution *provided*, with emphasis placed on that word, *provided* – because there is a chasm of difference in *knowing* the solution and *applying* it, just like *going* on a trip while *sitting* on your front porch!

Application will be our emphasis in this discussion. David, in describing his condition at the point found in Psalms 38, used such words as these: *Your arrows pierce me deeply; there is no soundness in my flesh; for my iniquities have gone over my head; like a heavy burden they are too heavy for me; I am troubled, I bow down greatly . . . .*

These words, selected at random in Psalm 38, describe the guilt-ridden King David.

THE CAUSE OF HIS GUILT

At the outset, we will consider what would cause such an awareness of guilt. Looking at the Old Testament legal system and sacrifices, we must ask why they did not resolve David's problem of guilt.

The answer is clearly given, as the inspired writer of the letter to the Hebrews observed, *For the law, having a shadow of good things to come, and not the very image of the things, can never with these same sacrifices . . . . make those who approach perfect.* (Hebrews 10: 1)

The point made here, by the inspired writer, makes it clear that the law and its accompanying sacrificial system was never intended to be more than a *shadow, a skia,* an outline or image of the perfect sacrifice to come. As we have previously emphasized, the law was our tutor, our schoolmaster to bring us to Christ. (Galatians 3: 24) The law was designed to bring conviction and guilt; the sacrificial system was an image, a fore-shadowing of the perfect solution that God would provide through Jesus, the Christ, the Anointed One.

For example: suppose you have a beautiful daughter, and a delightful young man comes along, handsome, wealthy, genteel, mature, and thoroughly dedicated to the Lord. You say to him, Let me show you a photograph of my daughter. Why do you do that? Do you show the photo to him so he will be able to say, *May I have that picture to carry and treasure? With such a picture I will never need to marry.*

Not on your life! You want him to realize how incomplete his life is without such a beautiful gal as your daughter, so that he will say, *How can I meet her? Oh, I can hardly wait to see her personally.*

Here was the purpose of the Old Testament sacrificial system. It was simply to picture God's redeeming work in such a form that the individual would be drawn to look forward to the perfect sacrifice, not so that he would be satisfied with just the picture, the imperfect.

Here was David's problem: The law had smitten him with guilt consciousness; he had obviously responded with proper sacrifices. (II Samuel 22: 5-7), yet he was still afflicted with guilt - sin consciousness still pervaded.

Why? Suppose we illustrate the answer. Suppose you have committed some terrible sin: murder, adultery, or theft. I say to you, I'm going to write your sin out on a chalkboard and display it before the entire congregation on Sunday morning. Finally, after you plead with me, I consent to take a cloth and cover the writing. So here it stands, right before a crowd of people. What are you thinking about? Your mind is on the words under the cover. What if someone peeks under the cover? What if it falls off, you think? You are consumed with guilt, despite the fact that those words are covered. That cover won't keep you from being smitten with guilt.

Now, let's look back to David: He has committed adultery with Bathsheba. He conspired and arranged the death of her husband, Uriah. He has lied, been deceitful. The Day of Atonement comes, and the animal sacrifice is offered that serves as a covering for his sin. But does that really take care of the guilt with which he is smitten? David realizes that the sin is still there, only covered. The more he thinks the more miserable he is.

> *It was symbolic for the present time in*
> *which both gifts and sacrifices are offered*
> *which cannot make him who performed the*
> *service perfect in regard to the conscience.*
> *(Hebrews 9: 9)*

David could cover it up, but the covering would not remove his guilty conscience.

The housewife may sweep a pile of dirt under the carpet so it cannot be seen by company, but she will not be able to walk on that carpet without thinking about the dirt under it.

THE GUILT PROBLEM SOLVED

David knew that the animal sacrifice was only a shadow of the perfect deliverance to come, but would look forward in faith which would bring perfect release. Thus he makes reference to the perfect solution God will provide.

> *Make haste to help me, O Lord, my*
> *salvation. (Psalm 38: 22)*

God's perfect solution provided is all wrapped up in that one big word – *salvation*. Everything that God has ever done and will ever do for man is packaged in that one word.

J. B. Phillips, in his book *Your God is Too Small*, presents the hypothesis that our view of God is too small. The same is true when it comes to that word *salvation*. Our concept of *salvation* is too small!

What comes to your mind when you hear that word? More often than not, you probably thought about *being saved* from eternal death and hell, about becoming a Christian.

Suppose we illustrate this limited view. Just imagine you are living in a hovel, have no money, and face imminent starvation. Even now the hunger pains gnaw away at you. Then someone comes along and says, *I'll give you money. Here is a draft order. Go and draw it from the bank.* Now, *money* may mean just enough provisions to furnish the basic essentials for food and clothing, meaning you will have to keep on living in the hovel. On the other hand, it could mean unlimited resources that would include a mansion on the hilltop, a silver cloud Rolls Royce, and a vacation trip around the world.

Salvation is like that. It is seen, more often than not, with a limited view: a deliverance from hell and death, but you must still live in a hovel to help pay for your sins; while in reality *salvation* includes escape from all past squalor, also including the mansion with all of the best furnishings: *love, joy, peace, longsuffering, gentleness, goodness, faith, meekness, temperance* . . . (Galatians 5: 22, 23)

Salvation equips you all of the way from regeneration, to sanctification, an abundant life, to glorification. (Romans 8: 28-30)

Notice, guilt is not a part of the furniture of life. The old ragged, miserable, uncomfortable couch of guilt has been hauled away to God's dump of forgetfulness!

The Old Testament provides the picture, the shadow, the type of things to come. The New Testament provides the completed article. What is included in this perfect solution now provided in Christ? One, the past with all of its failures is washed away; the old is made new. Initially, in response to faith, in a once for all action, sins are washed away. The Bible says, *The blood of Jesus Christ His son cleanses us from all sin,* (I John 1: 7) – or as the inspired writer to the Hebrews wrote, *We have been sanctified through the offering of the body of Jesus Christ once for all.* (Hebrews 10: 10)

Dealing specifically with guilt, we find these words from the Father: *how much more shall the blood of Christ, who through the eternal Spirit, offered Himself without spot to God, cleanse your conscience from dead words to serve the living God:* (Hebrews 9: 14), with the promise of a continued cleansing through God's word, as the Lord said, *Sanctify them by your truth. Your word is truth.* (John 17: 17) Finally, we see this invitation: *Let us draw near with a true heart in full assurance of faith, having our hearts sprinkled from an evil conscience and our bodies washed with pure water.* (Hebrews 10: 22)

Two, this new provision is permanently **sufficient**, never having to be repeated, as the inspired writer to the Hebrews writes; *But this Man [Jesus], after He had offered one sacrifice for sins forever, sat down at the right hand of God.* (Hebrews 10: 12)

The figure of Jesus' *sitting* down is an added indication that the task is completed. We sit down when we finish a job. God rested on the seventh day, not because He was tired, but because the task of creation was completed. The Lord Jesus *sat down at the right hand of God,* not because He was tired or resting, but because He had *forever* settled the sin and guilt problem. *For by one offering He has perfected forever those who are being sanctified.* (Hebrews 10: 14)

Three, the sin, guilt problem is so thoroughly **settled**, once one accepts God's cleansing, God does not even remember your sins, as we read, *Their sins and lawless deeds I will remember no more.* (Hebrews 10: 17). The removal of our sins is so far removed that we are told that our transgressions are removed from us *as far as the east is from the west.* (Psalm 103: 12). How far is that? A good answer comes in the old saying: *East is east, and west is west; and never the twain shall meet.*

Why, then, do we persist in feeling guilty?

CHAPTER ELEVEN

STUDY AND DISCUSSION GUIDE

1. What happens when man provides his own solution to the guilt problem, through his own efforts? Matthew 12: 43-45.

2. Read Titus 1: 16 and Isaiah 53: 6a, and discuss God's attitude toward man's dependence on his own works.

3. The hymn-writer wrote this question and answer: *What can wash away my sin? Nothing but the blood of Jesus.* This describes an approach to _____ sin and guilt in explaining it away. Read Job 8: 30-31, and discuss.

4. What was the cause of David's guilt, and its solution? Hebrews 10: 1; Galatians 3: 24; II Samuel 22: 5-7); Hebrews 9: 9.

5. The law and sacrifices were called a *shadow* of things to come in Hebrews 10: 1. Why was the law and sacrifices not sufficient in removing David's guilt? Hebrews 9: 9. Discuss extensively, considering the concept that David's guilt was covered (atoned).

CHAPTER TWELVE
PRIVATE ENEMY #3, GUILT, PART 4

The only solution to man's problems, including guilt, must come from God. How wonderful, then, as we discovered in our last chapter, that God has provided a perfect solution: *In Christ*, man's sordid past is abolished; sin is washed away, never to be remembered against us.

Now, a consideration of what will perhaps be the most important point in OUR consideration of guilt is the topic: God's perfect solution applied – the practical application of His solution.

THE PRACTICAL APPLICATION
We want to see and understand God's solution to the guilt problem, and how that solution can be practically applied for the individual, continuing to use King David as our chief example.

DESIRE
First, one must **desire** to be free of guilt, have the will and determination to accept God's solution.

One might think that desire should be automatic, but be reminded that some people seem to delight in wallowing in misery. They wear their miserable condition like an old dirty shirt, as they try to justify it.

Though I do not consider myself to be a counselor, I have spent thousands of hours giving counsel to people beset by problems. Amazingly, I suggest simple solutions, only to have those suggestions completely ignored, as their misery continues. One counseling session ends with solutions, only to begin with the same problem in the next session. Some people wear misery and guilt like a badge of honor, as though they delight in it.

The question is, then, if you are afflicted with guilt, do you have the desire and determination, the will to accept God's solution? David did, as we read his words, *For I will declare my iniquity; I will be in anguish over my sin…."* (Psalm 38: 18)

The tense of the verb *will* is in the present tense, meaning, *I will and I do declare my iniquity, and I am sorry for my sin.* David was determined to accept God's solution *now*, as he concludes later, *Make haste to help me, O Lord, my salvation."* (Psalm 38: 22). David said, *Lord, hurry up, I need help now!*

You see, until you bring your *I will* to the present tense, *I do*, your solution is hopeless, just in a morass of procrastination, continuing to wallow in your guilt like an old sow in a puddle of mud! This suggestion is not just the *power of positive thinking*, but you must *will*, be determined in your own mind *now*, if you are to succeed. Listen to the words of this poet:

> *If you think you'll lose, you're lost;*
> *For out in the world we find success begins*
> *With a fellow's will; it's all in the state of mind.*
> *(Thinking, W.D. Wentle)*

ACCEPT, VISUALIZE

Second, you must not only be willing to accept yourself as you are, but also **visualize what God wants you to be**, and what He can make of you.

David recognized himself as God's creation, but still knew that God had greater things for him. He said, as recorded in Psalm 139,

> *I will praise you [God], for I am fearfully*
> *And wonderfully made;*
> *Marvelous are your works, and that my soul*
> *knows very well. (Psalm 139: 14)*

Yet, David looked forward to further potential, what God could do in him, beyond what he was.

Search me, O God
And know my heart;
Try me, and know my anxieties (guilt?);
And see if there is any wicked way in me,
And lead me on the way everlasting.
(Psalm 139: 23-24)

Every person is two selves: the self he *is*, and the self he has the possibility of *becoming*.

THE SELF YOU ARE

First, realize that **the self you are**, as far as your ability, appearance, and aptitude are concerned, was designed by God, and *don't feel guilty for what you are not.*

Don't feel guilty about the job you are doing, as long as you have confidence that God has put you where you are. Robert Browning wrote in *Pippa Passes, All service ranks the same with God.*

Charles Allen had it right when he wrote these words: *It is not the work we do, but the spirit within us that determines our real lives. If work is done in the spirit of consecration, it is just as sacred to sell soap as it is to preach sermons . . .*

THE SELF YOU CAN BE

Next, be open to God's improvement, of what you are and what you do. Always be in search of a more excellent life and work. *But earnestly desire the best gifts. And yet I show you a more excellent way.* (I Corinthians 12: 31).

However, you must keep in mind that God may use trials, pressures, suffering, and even seeming failure in molding you into what He wants you to be. You must be careful not to wallow in self-misery and guilt as a result of these seeming defeats.

We are told that, by faith, Moses *refused to be called the son of Pharaoh's daughter.* What did he refuse? He was heir to the throne of Egypt, yet his decision was to defend his people, a decision that cost him his inheritance, causing him to flee for his life, resulting in a penniless state in the desert for 40 years. He became a sheepherder in the heat of the Sinai rather than a prince, and ended up suffering great affliction. (Hebrews 11: 24-27).

Moses could have been bitter over these losses, and defeated in guilt, saying I'm a flop, lower than a snake on hot pavement, but instead we read that he was *choosing rather to suffer affliction with the people of God than to enjoy the passing pleasures of sin.* (Hebrews 11: 25)

He permitted these pressures, and seeming defeat, to mold him into being God's great deliverer.

Yes, accept what you are, but always be responsive to, and seeking what God wants you to be. With this you will be able to take the next step.

GIVE YOURSELF TO GOD

If you are to defeat the problem of guilt, you must **give yourself into God's control.** As long as you retain possession of self, insist on self rights, God cannot work effectively in your life.

Every failure, every unhappiness, results from failure in meeting self-expectation. Self is not gratified in the way that you expected, and you are not willing to even consider the possibility that God has other expectations of *and* for you. Give yourself away to God and live the exciting adventure of being thrilled with God's provisions and challenges, rather than disappointment because self is not gratified. The Bible says, *Present your bodies a living sacrifice, holy, acceptable to God, which is your reasonable service.* (Romans 12: 1)

You are to present yourself *alive* to God, a gift that He can use as a living, viable instrument, like a fiddle in the hands of a master violinist. Any other relationship is unreasonable. A young woman went to the pastor of a large church in the south, and talked to him about a job in the church. When he asked what salary she expected, her reply was: *I will live on whatever I get. What I want is an opportunity to serve God.* She wanted to give herself as a *living sacrifice.*

When I came to the church which I pastored for almost 28 years, the 14 people who called me as Pastor said, *We can't offer you a salary, but will promise we won't let you starve to death.* I responded, *I'll be there next Sunday.* The lack of a salary, at that moment was unimportant. I felt as the Apostle Paul, *Woe is me if I preach not the gospel…*

Things changed the following week as I sat looking out over the weed patch in front of the little redwood building, part of which was supposed to be the parking lot, all spotted with gopher holes like a pair of worn-out blue-jeans. I thought to myself, *what am I doing here? How long will I have to stay before I can graciously leave?* I was unhappy. Why? My self-expectations were unfulfilled. Guilt as a result of supposed failure resulted; my ulcer began to bleed; I was as miserable as a young man in love, rejected by the girl of his dreams.

Then Sunday morning came, as I stood looking out behind a curtain, waiting to see if that *handful* of people would show up, while my ulcer throbbed. Then the Holy Spirit brought the words of Jesus to my mind, *But seek ye first the kingdom of God, and all these things shall be added to you.* (Matthew 6: 33, KJV). I gave myself to the Lord at that moment. I told Him, *God, this is your work. I'll do the best I can and leave the results to you.* What relief! My ulcer ceased throbbing, and joy of ministry came.

You must give yourself to God if you are to solve the guilt problem. Otherwise, you are a dead sacrifice, not a living sacrifice as required; and dead sacrifices compound guilt.

FAITH

As I have shared Christ with many over the years, I hear this question in response: How do I know that God will accept me? If you are to give yourself to God, you must have *faith* that He will accept the gift.

In addition, if you are to be free of guilt, **you must have faith** in the salvation He has provided, for as the Bible says, *Without faith it is impossible to please God.* (Hebrews 11: 6)

Faith is the catalyst that changes the riches of God into reality; the coinage that provides them as your personal possession; the bucket, when lowered into the well that brings forth the forgiving grace of God to refresh your soul. Jesus said to the father of the son whom His disciples could not heal, *If you can believe, all things are possible to him who believes.* (Mark 9: 23)

William James, the outstanding American philosopher, said that from a purely rational view, *In any project the one important factor is your belief. Without belief there can be no successful outcome. That is fundamental.*

Ralph Waldo Emerson said the same thing, just in different words. *Belief is absolutely necessary; no accomplishment, no assistance, no training can compensate for the lack of belief.*

Give yourself to God, and have faith that He accepts the gift. How can you know? Did He not ask you to give yourself to Him? Then, could He ask for the gift, and turn the giver away? Jesus invited, *Come to me, all you who labor and are heavy laden, and I will give you rest.* (Matthew 11: 28); or as He said, *The one who comes to me I will by no means cast out.* (John 6: 37)

Could God's son invite you to come, and then turn you away? Unthinkable! Visualize yourself in His presence by faith, and that presence will materialize. Accept His promise, as the Bible says, *Draw near to God and He will draw near to you.* (James 4: 8)

A young man, one among many, to whom I was ministering, prayed and asked the Savior to come into his life. After the prayer, I asked, *Did He come in?* He answered, *I don't know.* How could I give assurance to him in the light of that answer? I reminded him of the Savior's promise, *If anyone hears my voice and opens the door, I will come in to him. . .* (Rev. 3: 20). I asked, *Would Jesus lie to you?* The light came on, as he said, *ah, He did come in because He promised to do so if I asked!*

Just make practical application of God's promise and forever erase doubt from your life. John Bunyan wrote in his book, *Holy City, only faith can make Satan flee. O, the toil of a gracious heart in this combat if faith is weak! The man can get no higher than his knees, until an arm from heaven helps him up.*

Claim the promise found in the book of *James,* chapter four, verse ten:

> *Humble yourselves in the sight of the Lord,*
> *And He will lift you up.*

REMOVE THE BASIS FOR GUILT

There is one final step in removing guilt from life and that is, remove the basis or cause of the guilt.

ACCEPT CHRIST

The first step in removing the basis for guilt is by the **acceptance of Christ** as Savior and Lord.

Here is the beginning place for every person. *All have sinned* (Romans 3: 23); and *the penalty for sin is death*, eternal and spiritual (Romans 6: 23). Sin is the basis, the cause of guilt.

The only solution and way to avoid sin's penalty, death, is to accept God's remedy: receive the Lord Jesus Christ as Savior. Bypass that solution to the sin-death problem, and even if you make application of some of the other steps I mention, it will be like trying to remove cancer by taking an aspirin.

Jesus said, *I am the way, the truth, and the life. No one comes to the Father except through me.* (John 14: 6). There is no way of solving the sin-guilt problem without first going through Jesus Christ as Savior. The poet has written,

> *I must needs go home by the*
> *way of the cross,*
> *there's no other way but this.*

CONFESSION

The second step in removing the basis, the cause of guilt, is **confession.** God makes only one requirement of the believer for the eradication of your guilt toward Him. That solution is found in these words:

> *If we confess our sins, He [God] is*
> *faithful and just to forgive us our sins*
> *and to cleanse us from all unrighteousness.*
> *(I John 1: 9)*

A more complete understanding of this promise comes as we read this Proverb:

He who covers his sins will not prosper,
*But whoever confesses **and forsakes***
them will have mercy. (Proverbs 28: 13)

Confession of sin [to God], with the intention of forsaking it, brings absolute forgiveness and cleansing. You don't have to crawl to church over broken glass; you don't have to fast, sitting in sack-cloth and ashes, rend your body, gnash your teeth, and plead for 72 hours; you don't have to sit in a confessional booth or do penance. God says simply, *he who confesses and forsakes his sin will have mercy*!

David obviously knew this truth as we hear him proclaim, *For I will declare my iniquity; I will be in anguish (sorrow) over my sin.* (Psalm 38: 18). That he did so and found release is obvious, as we further read these words:

Blessed is he whose transgression is
forgiven, whose sin is covered. Blessed
is the man to whom the Lord does not
impute iniquity, and in whose spirit there
is no deceit. (Psalm 32: 1-2)

Time and again the guilt-laden have sought my counsel, have applied First John 1:9 by faith, and have arisen to exclaim, what freedom! What release! It works!

However, there are those who have a guilt problem because of a faulty relationship with another person. This problem must first be resolved, no matter who is at fault. If you have offended your brother, Jesus said, *If you bring your gift to the altar and there remember that your brother has something against you, leave your gift there before the altar, and go your way. First be reconciled to your brother, and then come and offer your gift.* (Matthew 5: 23-24)

On the other hand, if another has offended you, the initiative is still yours. Remember, Peter asked the Master, *Lord, how often shall my brother sin against me, and I forgive him? Up to seven times? Jesus said to him, 'I do not say to you, up to seven times, but up to seventy times seven.'*

How is this reconciliation accomplished? The greater relationship with God illustrates the lesser relationship with man. Confession is the answer! Admit your wrong without an alibi; seek reconciliation, then if restitution is indicated, do that. Zaccheus, up the sycamore tree in Jericho, found forgiveness from Jesus; but also found that a four-fold restitution was in order. As Zaccheus said, *If I have taken anything from anyone by false accusation, I restore four-fold.* (Luke 19: 8)

God's word makes it clear that His forgiveness only comes as we are willing to forgive and correct wrong relationships, *For if you forgive men their trespasses,* Jesus said, *Your heavenly Father will also forgive you.* Furthermore, He added, *if you do not forgive men their trespasses, neither will your Father forgive your trespasses.* (Matthew 6: 14-15)

RENEW YOUR MIND

The third step in removing the cause of guilt is by the **renewing of your mind.** The Apostle Paul wrote, *be transformed by the renewing of your mind.* (Romans 12: 2). In other words, change your life by changing the content of your mind - your thoughts.

How does one go about renewing the mind? First, by faith, you fill it with God's word. Wash your mind with the water of God's word; and fill it with the same cleansing content.

Next, act on the word when you put it there. Knowledge without application can be a dangerous thing. The importance of application is given by James as he admonishes, *be doers of the word and not hearers only, deceiving yourselves.* (James 1: 22). If you hear, and don't apply what you hear, James says that you *are like a man observing his natural face in a mirror . . . goes away, and immediately forgets what kind of man he was.* (James 1: 23-24). *Let this mind be in you*, Paul wrote to the Philippians, *which was also in Christ Jesus.* (Philippians 2: 5). No room there for guilt!

Isaiah wrote, *You [God] will keep him in perfect peace, whose mind is stayed on you, because he trusts in you.* (Isaiah 26: 3). That word *stayed* is the Hebrew word samak which means *to sustain or support.* So God promises to liberate you to peace, if you will only permit Him to support or sustain your mind – in renewal and trust.

PRACTICE HOLY LIVING

A fourth step in removing the basis, the cause of guilt is by *practicing holy living*.

As Paul made his defense before Governor Felix, he said, *I have hope in the resurrection of the dead. This being so I myself always strive to have a conscience without offense toward God and men.* (Acts 24: 16). That adds up in striving to live a holy life.

The Apostle writes, *For God did not call us to uncleanness, but in holiness.* (1 Thess. 4: 7)

CONCLUSION

We would close this consideration with the reminder that all will be to no avail if you miss the first step: the new birth through faith in the Lord Jesus Christ!

My mentor, Bob Cheek, told the story, and I read it again in more detail in a sermon by the evangelist, Angel Martinez. I close this section on guilt with this story as told by Angel Martinez, authenticated by historical record.

In Martinez's sermon, *Play Ball*, he likened life to a baseball game, naming first base *salvation*, second base *baptism* and church membership, third base *Christian Service*, and fourth base or home base as *Heaven*. Then comes the story:

The setting was the world series of 1924 between Washington and New York. The series was tied three games each. The last game would decide the series being played in Washington.

Washington was up to bat in the last half of the ninth inning. The score was tied two all. One run would win the game and the series.

The first two men up to bat made routine outs. Then a batter by the name of Goose Goslin came to bat. The count reached two balls and two strikes. On the fifth pitch Goslin stepped into the ball and slammed it into deep left-center field, just missing clearing the fence for a home run by 6 inches.

As Goslin came to third base with a triple, the coach waved him home in an effort to stretch the hit to a home run and win the game.

Goslin slid into home plate with a cloud of dust. The play was close. Moments later the umpire extended his thumb and proclaimed, *you're out!*

The crowd was furious. Goslin appeared to be safe. Then moments after conferring with the other umpires, the home-plate umpire gave the final decision to the raging crowd: *Ladies and gentlemen, the man at home plate is out **because he didn't touch first base!*** A true story! (Checked by me in the reference section at the public library)

Jesus said, *Most assuredly, I say to you, unless one is born again, he cannot see the kingdom of God.* (John 3: 3)

Just as one cannot score in a baseball game without touching first base; one cannot be saved and go to heaven without receiving Jesus Christ as Savior.

CHAPTER TWELVE

STUDY AND DISCUSSION GUIDE

1. In taking God's solution for guilt, you should not feel guilty for what you are, but you should do what?
1 Corinthians 12: 31; Hebrews 11: 24-27.

2. Read Romans 12: 1 and discuss what is meant by giving yourself to God.

3. If you give yourself to God, how do you know He accepts the gift? Matthew 11: 28; John 6: 37.

4. What is the first step in removing the basis or cause for guilt? (Romans 3: 23; Romans 6: 23; John 14: 6.

5. What is the second step in removing the cause for guilt? John 1: 9; Proverbs 28: 13; Psalm 38:18; psalm 32: 1-2.

6. How can you renew your mind? Romans 12: 2; James 1: 23-24; Philippians 2: 5.

7. Retell the Goose Goslin baseball story and make application. John 3: 3.

CHAPTER THIRTEEN

SPIRITUAL ENEMY #4, DISCOURAGEMENT

DEFEATING THE PROBLEMS OF LIFE

Never under-estimate your enemy, is an adage well worth taking to heart; and an enemy which I am convinced is badly underestimated is that of *discouragement*, or just plain *depression*. How many lives are defeated; how many are robbed of joy; how many souls perish because of defeat by discouragement?

The word appears very few times in the English Bible, but we find many forms and synonyms in the original Hebrew and Greek, translated in such descriptive terms as: *affliction, anguish, distress, defeat, cast down, grief, oppression, sadness, sorrow, pain*, and on and on it goes. The words come in great variety; they just add up to much the same meaning. In our daily vocabulary there are: *blue Mondays*; and statements like these: *I don't know what is wrong with me, I just feel down; is life really worth living?; the whole world is against me; does God really care* – all manifesting discouragement, depression, dejection, despair, defeat, d, d, d . . . all those d's that rob the Christian of joy and productivity.

Do you begin to see how this dread enemy afflicts, battles, bruises, wounds you almost every day, like an incipient headache that refuses to go away? How productive are you when you have the *blues*, are in the *dumps*, weary and dejected – the plain old spiritual blues?

I hope I can show you, in part at least, how to defeat the problem of discouragement; and as the poet says, *Get on the sunny side of the street!*

Back in the great band era, I loved the orchestra directed by Tommy Dorsey. Tommy had a number, as best I remember, that went something like this:

> *You can walk in the shade*
> *with your blues on parade. . .*
> *(or the alternative)*
> *just direct your feet*
> *to the sunny side of the street.*

Defeat the problem of discouragement through Christ. The choice is yours, as Dorsey's song says, *You can walk in the shade with your blues on parade* or you can *direct your feet to the sunny side of the street!*

HOW NOT TO DEFEAT DISCOURAGEMENT

Let me begin by telling you *how not* to defeat discouragement: not by pills, psychiatrists, pleasure, plenty, the panaceas of the world.

YOU CAN'T SLEEP IT OFF

First, you can't sleep off discouragement or depression with the sleep of the world. Have you ever been burdened, cast down, have the blahs, and in an effort to escape just gone to bed to sleep? Silly boy or girl, sure you have! You are an unusual person if you have not.

But sleep hasn't provided the solution, has it? It's still there when you wake up, and now you are groggy and fuzzy headed!

Let me illustrate this truth from the scriptures. Remember how Jesus told His disciples of His impending betrayal and death when He went to Gethsemane in anguish, asking them to watch and pray with Him. What did they do? Read what happened:

> *When He rose from His prayer, and had*
> *come to His disciples, He found them*
> *sleeping from sorrow. (Luke 22: 46)*

Was this a proper solution? Jesus said to them, *Why do you sleep,* indicating in His question their failure. (Luke 22: 46)

Second, you cannot drown your sorrows; relieve your discouragement, dejection, depression, or weariness by the intoxicating drinks, the *wine* of the world.

Solomon wrote in the book off *Ecclesiastes* about how he had endeavored to solve his problems with wine, women and song, riches, power, knowledge, and ended up with this conclusion:

> *I have seen all the works that are done*
> *under the sun; and indeed all is vanity and*
> *grasping for the wind. (Ecclesiastes 1: 14)*

He indicates that, trying to solve the problem with solutions from the world, is like *grasping for the wind.* Have you ever tried to grab a handful of wind?

He added in Ecclesiastes 2: 20: *Therefore I turned my heart and despaired of all the labor in which I toiled under the sun.* That phrase, *turned my heart and despaired* corresponds to the Latin *despondet aninum,* meaning that he gave up his spirit and let it sink, i.e., he despairs.

All that the world has to offer is like *grasping for the wind* and ends in despair – *despondet aninum!*

The Bible says,

> *For all that is in the world – the lust of*
> *the flesh, the lust of the eyes, and the pride*
> *of life – is not of the Father but is of the*
> *world. (I John 2: 16)*

One needs only recall the rich young ruler who came to the Savior searching for the way to life. He was rich; as we are told that *he had great possessions.* He was a good moral man, as he replied about his obedience to the commandments governing man's relations with man, all *these things I have kept from my youth.* Yet, *he went away sorrowful.* (Matthew 19: 16-22).

Riches, power, morality, reputation and whatever else the world could offer brought no remedy. He was still *sad* – a bad case of discouragement!

C. S. Lewis, in his book *Mere Christianity*, sums up the hope-lessness of depending on the world, and points us in the right direction with these words:

> *Aim at heaven and you will get earth*
> *thrown in. Aim at earth and you get neither.*

THE SOLUTION
KNOW GOD'S WORD

One, know God's word, as it reveals His perfect plan for your life, and how to put His plan for your life into operation.

This knowledge comes through *Bible study*. Listen to the words of the Psalmist in Psalm 119. Look first to verse 25, where we see the *problem*: *My soul clings to the dust*. That's real depression! Then the *solution* is given immediately, *Revive me according to Your word*. Next, move to verse 28, where he begins with the *problem*: *My soul melts from heaviness*. The word *melts* is the Hebrew word *dalaph* which means *to drop* or be *depressed*! Again the immediate *solution*: *Strengthen me according to Your word*.

Suppose we look at some of the causes of discouragement, as we consider how to apply this solution:

First, discouragement or depression results from fear and un-certainty, as we are told *we must master fear through faith*. We are guided to victory over this fear by God's word, knowing as the Bible says,

> *So then faith comes by hearing,*
> *and hearing by the word of God.*
> *(Romans 10: 17)*

The lost sheep which has wandered from the fold is inclined to be consumed with fear, that because he wandered, the shepherd does not care for him. The individual who is sick in sin is cast down,

136

thinking that, because he is sick the Great Physician does not care for him.

God's word guides us out of the morass of such thoughts which discourage and depress, assuring us of His care, concern and compassion. Remember, as Jesus was commissioning His disciples to go out into fearful circumstances, the kinds that depress the soul, He described those circumstances in such words as these:

> Beware of men, for they will deliver you
> up to councils and scourge you in their
> synagogues.
> . . . . . .
> Brother will deliver up brother to death,
> and a father his child; and children will rise
> up against parents and cause them to be
> put to death. (Matthew 10: 17, 21)

These are pretty depressing circumstances, yet listen to these words of assurance that follow hard on their heels:

> Are not too sparrows sold for a copper
> coin? And not one of them falls to the
> ground apart from your Father's will. Do
> not fear therefore; you are of more value
> than many sparrows. (Matthew 10: 29, 31)

The Bible tells us that He is our heavenly Father, Who waits and guides His prodigal home; the Good Shepherd who goes in search for one lost sheep; the One who does not permit even a sparrow to escape His attention.

He cares for you to such an extent that even the hairs on your head are numbered. (Matthew 10: 30). How can you be discouraged by fear and uncertainty in the face of such care?

Next, discouragement comes when we try to contemplate the future, and are burdened by unsolved problems and overwhelming tasks.

Nothing depresses me more than to sit and contemplate my future schedule, more true when in my pastoral ministry: sermon preparation, Bible study, counseling, visitation, administration, preaching, teaching, conferences, meetings, problems, those who "just drop by or call up," my family responsibilities and personal life. Whew! I'm depressed just in making the list!

There is not enough time. I think of material needs: money is short and then news comes that Andrew needs a new pair of glasses, Jeanie a new bridge from the dentist, tuition for schooling and registration, some new tires, another dental appointment! I bow under the load, like a gnat flying against a windstorm, and because I don't have the resources and the time to do it all, I am discouraged and tempted to ditch it all!

Then I am reminded of the words of my Savior, *seek first the kingdom of God and His righteousness, and all these things shall be added to you.* (Matthew 6: 33). *All things, Lord?* Yes, all things!

So, I move on to the next part of His statement, as He admonishes me, *Therefore do not worry about tomorrow, take just one day at a time, for tomorrow will worry about its own things. Sufficient for the day is its own trouble.* (Matthew 6: 34)

It isn't today that discourages me so much; it is all of the tomorrows that I try to fit into today, feeling like those days when we were trying to squeeze all of the seven members of my family, including David, Danny, and Christopher Newton into my old VW Bug! Even if we succeeded, a lot of discomfort resulted. Just ask the kids!

Live joyfully and confidently, one day at a time, is our Lord's advice.

Again, discouragement results from pessimistic consideration of all that is wrong, without seeing the good. The country is going to pot; the national debt is threatening our nation's survival. The President won't defend DOMA. Only *bad news* is *good news* as far as the mass media is concerned. Violence rages in London, and that dominates headlines across the country; but 30,000 Christians gather to pray in Houston, Texas at Governor Perry's invitation, and the only news items about that you can find, are accusations that the Governor is violating the separation of church and state!

We are trained to see the shadows and not the sunshine; the chasms but not the bridges; the abyss and not the mountain top; the hate but not the love; the hopelessness but not the hope. We can't get our eyes off of the bad, and are defeated.

Then we look up, for God provides the solution: *Only fear the Lord, and serve Him in truth with all your heart; for consider what great things He has done for you.* (I Samuel 12: 24). Start in *Genesis* with creation, procreation; and go right on through to *Revelation*, including salvation and ultimate glorification. Yes! Yes! *Consider what great things He has done for you!*

Helen Keller was deaf and blind from the age of two, but when Yousef Karsh, a portrait photographer photographed her, he said, *The light came from within*, seeing the brightness of her hope. Speaking with Helen, he said, *Now having met you, I shall think of you in terms of sunrise.*

Helen Keller replied, *I wish that all men would take sunrise for their slogan, and leave the shadows of sunset behind them.*

As Tommy Dorsey's song said, *Leave your worries on the doorstep, just direct your feet to the sunny side of the street.*

Why do people choose to walk in the shadows of life? God gives His children the ability to leave the shadows, as we read, *Walk in the light . . . for God is light, and in Him is no darkness at all.* (I John 1: 7, 5)

Two, you must *act* on God's word; just knowing the solutions is not enough. You can have a million dollars in the bank, but live like a pauper by failing to draw on your account.

We are told that we can have perfect peace, just by keeping our mind on the Lord, because we trust in Him. (Isaiah 26: 3-4). But take note: we don't get the peace apart from keeping our eyes on and trusting Him.

ACT ON GOD'S WORD

The next part of the solution for depression is: Act on and draw on God's resources, and trust in His promises. Danger, trials, sickness may come; but they should only compel us to take the wings of the Spirit, driving us to the arms of the Great Physician.

PRAYER

Prayer is the first thing that comes to mind, when we think about acting and drawing on God. Of course such a conclusion is totally true and proper, as we look at this admonition:

> *Let us therefore come boldly to the throne*
> *of grace, that we may obtain mercy and*
> *find grace to help in time of need.*
> *(Hebrews 4: 16)*

We have often called Bible study and prayer the two parts of a healthy Christian heart beat: Bible study the *lub*, and prayer the *dub-dub-dub*. Couple sincere prayer with knowledge and application of God's word, and discouragement is impossible.

King Saul had pursued David relentlessly, in an effort to kill him, but God had wonderfully delivered David. Famine came upon the land for three years; war with the Philistines blighted the country; and still God wonderfully preserved David. So it is that we read how David knew prayer to be the answer. David said,

> *The sorrows of sheol surrounded me;*
> *the snares of death confronted me.*
> *(II Samuel 22: 6)*
> *Then came the answer: In my distress*
> *I called upon the Lord and cried out to*
> *my God; He heard my voice from His*
> *temple, and my cry entered His ears.*
> *(II Samuel 22: 7).*

In my distress: David said, *I called upon the Lord.* David knew that God would lift him up from his discouragement and depression, as he said, *He heard my voice . . . and my cry entered His ears.*

It is William Cowper who so beautifully expressed this truth in verse:

> *What various hindrances we meet in*
> *Coming to the mercy-seat!*
> *Yet who that knows the worth of prayer,*
> *But wishes to be often there!*
> *Prayer makes the darkened clouds withdraw,*
> *Prayer climbs the ladder Jacob saw,*
> *Gives exercise to faith and love,*
> *Brings every blessing from above.*
>
> *Restraining prayer, we cease to fight,*
> *Prayer makes the Christian's armor bright;*
> *And Satan trembles when he sees*
> *The weakest saint upon his knees.*
>
> *While Moses stood with arms open wide,*
> *Success was found on Israel's side;*
> *But when, through weariness they failed,*
> *That Amalek prevailed.*

It is hard for the devil to depress a saint on his knees in the presence of God!

FELLOWSHIP

Another ingredient needed in defeating discouragement is the fellowship of the saints in the church – the Koinonia. I do not believe that any Christian can live a victorious, discouragement-free life apart from the exhortation of fellow saints, as required in their assembly together, as we are admonished, *not forsaking*

141

the assembling of ourselves together, as is the manner of some, where we are told we are to be *exhorting one another . . .* (Hebrews 10: 25). It is here that we *bear one another's burdens, and so fulfill the law of Christ.* (Galatians 6: 21).

I can feel as low as a snake's bottom side, and come to church and be raised to the proverbial *cloud nine*!

TRUST GOD

The next thing in defeating discouragement is in simply trusting God and His promises. At times it may seem hard to trust God, due to all of the problems that surround us, making it seem as though God doesn't care, or is not even there. But as the old Southern Baptist Preacher, Vance Havner, said: *The **unseen hand** [of God] may be obscured at times by the fogs of circumstances, but **because we cannot see the sun on a cloudy day doesn't mean that it isn't there.*** Havner then added, *We can trust God's heart when we cannot trace His hand.*

In trusting Him, depend on His promises. Then, just continue by resting daily in that faith and trust, what we can call *faith-rest.* The inspired writer in Hebrews, chapter four, speaks of the failure of the Israelites to enter into God's rest, failing to claim His promise of rest for them. We read in verse 12:

> For indeed the gospel was preached to us
> as well as to them; but the word which they
> heard did not profit them, not being mixed
> with faith in those who heard it. (Hebrews 4: 2)

They failed in finding rest in God's promises because, as the tense in the Greek word has it, they failed to *keep on mixing* the promises of God's word with faith. So, if we are to find rest and defeat discouragement, we must *keep on mixing our faith with the Lord's promises.*

God stands ready to give us rest in response to faith, and there can be no discouragement where there is His rest. We can rest because our needs are provided by our Heavenly Father. One has said that God has made over 7,000 promises for the believer in time – not considering eternal provisions.

God had provided everything and it is ours, ours if we just keep mixing it with faith. God rested the seventh day from all His works, not because He was tired, but because His creative work was complete. So, we read concerning ourselves, *There remains therefore a rest for the people of God.* (Hebrews 4: 9)

Paul knew all about this faith-rest, in spite of going through intense suffering. He wrote:

> *We are hard pressed on every side, yet*
> *not crushed; we are perplexed, but not in*
> *despair; persecuted, but not forsaken;*
> *struck down, but not destroyed.*

Such is a list of the trials faced. In spite of it all, he adds, *Therefore we do not lose heart. Even though our outward man is perishing, yet the inward man is being renewed day by day.* (2 Corinthians 4: 8,9,16). Just keep on mixing it all with faith.

CONCLUSION

I finish with this account of a man named Harry, who wrote his life story under the title, *My Wheelchair To The Stars.*

Harry had rheumatic fever at the age of seven, later developing severe arthritis. His pain was so excruciating that just wearing his clothes was often torture. He began to feel that there was little reason to live.

One day when both of his parents were away working, he fell out of his chair and lay helplessly on the floor for several hours. Eventually the postman came, picked him up, and said to him, among other things, *Harry, with God all things are possible.* (Mark 10: 27)

These words burned themselves into Harry's mind. They drove out the black waves of bitterness.

Someone suggested that he paint Christmas cards. He worked 6 months making his first card that would sell for a nickel. Keeping trying, in one year he made $800 from his greeting cards.

Through a number of efforts, including a mortgage on his parents' home for $2,800.00, he financed a greeting card mail order business. His mother asked, *If you don't sell the cards that you have bought, what then?* Harry's answer came from God through that postman from years past: *with God all things are possible.*

He sold the cards!

Harry said that he would never forget the first year he had a million dollars worth of business; and he said, *I went to the stars in a wheelchair.*

Harry ended his story with thanksgiving to God for his struggles, through which God had enabled him to succeed.

Some of you may be cast down, discouraged, depressed and defeated, although you have all of your faculties intact, are not in a wheelchair, and may have two cars in the garage. We then ask,

Why are you cast down, O my soul?
And why are you disquieted within me?
Hope in God, for I shall yet praise Him
for the help of His countenance. (Psalm 42: 5)

CHAPTER THIRTEEN

STUDY AND DISCUSSION GUIDE

1. Is sleep a good solution in dealing with discouragement? Luke 22: 45-46. Discuss

2. Can you drown your discouragement with things of the world? Ecclesiastes 1: 14, 2: 20; I John 2: 16

3. We find in Psalm 119: 25-28 that knowledge of God's word is a solution to discouragement. Read and discuss.

4. We said that discouragement often comes from fear and uncertainty. What is its solution? Romans 16: 17; Matthew 10: 17, 21, 29, 31. Discuss.

5. Why do your thoughts about the future cause you to be discouraged? What is the solution? Matthew 6: 33, 34.

6. What is the first thing we think about when acting on a problem? Hebrews 4: 16; II Samuel 22: 6-7.

7. What is the next action after prayer in dealing with discouragement? Hebrews 10: 25; Galatians 6: 2.

8. What is the final step in the conquest of discouragement? Hebrews 4: 2, 9; II Corinthians 4: 8, 9, 16.

CHAPTER FOURTEEN
SET PRIORITIES

What is *your* greatest need, as you consider dealing with these Personal Enemies? A gentleman selling motivational success plans asked this question of me. He anticipated a specific problem in my answer, hoping for an area into which he could get his teeth, in demonstrating how his program would solve my need, all in order to make a sale.

My biggest need, I answered, is *more time. . . I just need more time to do all the work I have to do. If you can tell me how to get 48 hours in a day, we can do business.*

Needless to say, that was not the response he wanted. He finally gave up in despair when I failed to narrow my need to a specific problem area. However, I was honest. I just didn't have enough time to do everything that needed to be done.

What can *we* do with that problem? How can we narrow that into a workable solution? Right away you and I know that we can't add 24 hours to a day – and we wouldn't have the energy to use it, if we could!

SOLUTION

The only solution is for us to carefully *set priorities*, and do the most important things first. Here is what my salesman friend was coaxing me to do, set a priority so he could provide a motivational scheme for reaching it. So, I guess I should have told him that, *setting priorities was my biggest problem and need*; and that is precisely our need at this point, in response to the lessons we have been learning in this book.

How about you? What is your biggest need? One might honestly say, as an example, *I'm too absorbed with making money.* A young guy might reply, *Girls are my area of focus*. Get the idea? How are you really using your best time?

I really struggle in this area. See, I'm being honest, letting it all hang out. My associate would say (in years past): *Pastor you need physical exercise.* I say, *You are right;* and right away he wants me out on the athletic field jogging! My wife says, *Hon, you need to spend more time with your boys. You need to be teaching them . . . showing them . . . working with them.* She's right, and I know it. Here is another tremendous need. Why don't I do it today? When will I get around to it, if ever?

Then I preach a series of messages on prayer, and I'm con-victed that I need to spend more time in prayer. Martin Luther said that he had so much to do at times that he couldn't possibly get by without at least 5 hours a day in prayer!

I know it! I know it! I need to spend more time with my family, for exercise, for prayer, for study, for soul winning . . . but I don't have any more time. That nice salesman could not put an addi-tional 24 hours in a day . . . what can I do?

There is only one sensible response: **work on priorities**. I would say to school graduates: Learn how to carefully set priori-ties if you want to succeed in life. Determine where you *ought* to go, *want* to go, and lay careful plans for getting there. Set goals; lay plans for achieving them; *check up* on your goals and plans regularly; adjust where adjustments are needed – and you can have a fulfilling life! Hey! I need to practice what I preach! So, let's do it together

We need to start with Jesus' suggestion in the following scripture. Have single vision. Set our sights on the right goal, and not get side-tracked. Get our priorities in order. We need to read Matthew 6: 19-24 and apply it to our life!

> *For where your treasure (your priority)*
> *is, there your heart (your affections) will be*
> *also. (Matthew 6: 21)*

My aim: I want to show you how to determine what your priorities *are*: and how to set the right ones. Your answers will come from Matthew 6: 19-24. Nothing complicated; nothing profound; just a simple exercise and application of God's word that anyone can do, as simple as taking a breath of fresh air!

DETERMINING YOUR PRIORITIES
YOUR ACTIVITIES

One, your *activities* will tell you what is priority in your life right now. The Lord Jesus said, *Do not lay up for yourselves treasures on earth, where moth and rust destroy and thieves break in and steal; but lay up for yourselves treasures in heaven, where neither moth nor rust destroys and where thieves do not break through and steal.* (Matthew 6:19, 20) In other words, set your priorities on those things of eternal value which endure, rather than focusing on the material and carnal, which are at best, temporary.

Have you ever made an analysis to determine what you spend your life doing – the activities of your life? People do the things they want to do. Take time right now and make a list of the activities that consume your time, things other than absolute necessities.

Now look at your inventory. Do you need to alter your list?

Two, your *anxieties* will tell you what concerns you most. (Read Matthew 6: 25-30). Jesus says repeatedly in this passage, *Do not worry; don't be anxious* about life, food, drink, clothing (Matthew 6: 25).

Note carefully: He isn't saying, as some might suggest, that you should just sit and do nothing, and not care. No, no! He is saying, you can go to work; just don't let anxiety eat you up!

The things about which you are anxious *are* your priorities – your greatest concern. You don't agree? Listen, if they are not important to you, you won't be anxious. You are anxious about them because they are on the top of your list.

Now, look back at your list. Take a few moments to think about those things about which you are most concerned (anxious). Do you need to alter your list? Jesus refers to treasures: life, drink, clothing, food. One person might say: food, fashion and finance.

What are you concerned about? Answer that, and you will have determined some priorities – right or wrong. And no matter what they are, don't be anxious about them, because you can't change them through anxiety. As Jesus asked, *Which of you by being anxious can grow 18" taller?* (Matthew 6: 27), You protest: Jesus didn't say anything about 18 inches! Yes, He did! He used the word *cubit*, which is the length between the elbow and the tip your hand, approximately 18 inches. However, the length used is irrelevant. You can't grow a tenth of an inch taller through anxiety, even if you gnash your teeth and beat your chest!

Then the Master talks about birds and how God feeds them; about flowers and how God clothes them; and emphasizes that, if you will get your priorities in order, He will take care of those food and clothing needs! (Matthew 6: 33) Again, anxiety about *anything* has no place in the believer's life.

A third thing that will reveal your priorities are your *ambitions*. As our Lord said,

> *For after all these things the Gentiles*
> *seek [are ambitions for them]. (Matthew 6: 32)*

Oh yes, you should be ambitious, that is, to fulfill the God-given purpose for your life. But what about *your* ambition?

At one point in my life, as a boy, my greatest ambition was to be a professional baseball player. Other times in my life I just wanted to eat, drink, and be merry. At these times I gave no consideration of God's plan in my ambitions.

What goals do you hope to accomplish? What are your ambitions? Look at your list again. Do you need to make any changes?

Now, some of the things you have written down may be important, but should they rate so high on your list?

YOUR PRIORITY/S

Is your relationship with God, and His plan for your life, your number one priority, as it should be? Jesus said,

But seek first the kingdom of God and His righteousness . . . (Matthew 6: 33) - and when you put Him first, all things else fall into their rightful place - and all these things shall be added to you.

This promise enriched and transformed my life at its discovery and application!

The only kingdom of God, on this earth right now, is within the man in whose heart Christ reigns as King. The only way you can seek the kingdom of God, which is top priority, is to seek His rule and control over your life . . . as owner, Ruler, Master, Lord, and King. . . . . *The Kingdom of God is within you.* (Luke 17: 21)

A PERSONAL RELATIONSHIP

You must begin with a personal *relationship*. The priority of priorities is to make sure that the King is within, on the throne of your life. How can one be sure? The words of the Savior to Nicodemus give us our answer. Jesus said, *Most assuredly I say to you, Unless one is born again, he cannot see the kingdom of God.* (John 3: 3)

The spiritual birth begins by simply placing the King on the throne of your life by faith. You say, *Lord, move in and take over; be my Savior and Lord of my life.*

The priority of priorities, regarding the Kingdom of God, begins with the new birth. So be sure the King is on the throne of your life!

A RULER

You continue your new life with Christ as *Ruler*, after establishing the relationship. Don't slide Him off the throne and replace Him with self. Permit Him to rule your life on a moment by moment basis, as Paul wrote to the Romans, *for the kingdom of God is not eating and drinking, but righteousness and peace and joy in the Holy Spirit.* (Romans 14: 17).

We read again, *For the kingdom of God is not in word but in power.* (I Corinthians 4: 20). The marks of the kingdom are: right-

151

eousness, peace, joy – a new life style, not (just) in word but in power – God's mighty power!

If the King is on the throne, His power will show through your life. Your priority should be the demonstration of this power to others, resulting in the expansion of the Kingdom . . . with new subjects!

CONCLUSION

Your, our priority should be as Christ's model prayer requests, *your Kingdom come* . . . (Matthew 6: 10); Pray," [Lord Jesus], *your kingdom come* - in my life through the reign of Christ through the new birth; in my life through the continuing and expanding rule of Christ; in the lives of others as God's power, through me, *reaches* out to touch and transform others in both word and deed.

Seek Him first; live for Him; and He will arrange the other things for you!

Apply these words, as written by the Apostle Paul to the Romans, and you will have the assurance that you are *more than conquerors* throughout every problem in life!

> Yet in all these things **we are more than conquerors** <u>through Him who loved us</u>. For I am persuaded that neither death nor life, nor angels nor principalities nor powers, nor things present nor things to come, nor height nor depth, nor any other created thing, shall be able to separate us from the love of God which is in Christ Jesus our Lord. (Romans 8: 37-39)

CHAPTER FOURTEEN

STUDY AND DISCUSSION GUIDE

Application of what you learned

put into practice the steps found in this chapter!

Acknowledgements

Again I am greatly indebted to **Sally Mattos**, who masterfully interpreted my hand-written manuscript, copied it on her computer's hard drive, e-mailing it back to me chapter by chapter, where I edited and proofed the final product that you hold in your hand. I am fearful that I may have never completed the task without Sally's help.

Furthermore, I must give credit to **Create Space,** an **Amazon.com** company, who cooperated beautifully in producing this book in its final form.

Finally, a word of thanks to my church, **Gateway Bible Church,** for encouragement and for permitting me to market the book through the church